SO-CLZ-667

The ITT Key Issues Lecture Series

is made possible through a grant
from ITT Corporation

This series of lectures took place
from October, 1982 to April, 1983 at
The Owen Graduate School of Management,
Vanderbilt University in Nashville, Tennessee.

THE
AMERICAN WORK FORCE:
Labor and Employment
in the 1980's

Edited by

Robert A. Ullrich
Professor of Management
Owen Graduate School of Management
Vanderbilt University

With a Foreword by

Rand V. Araskog
Chairman and President
ITT Corporation

Pfeiffer Library
Pfeiffer College
Misenheimer, N. C. 28109

DISCARD

 *Auburn House Publishing Company*
Dover, Massachusetts

124183

Copyright © 1984 by Auburn House Publishing Company.

All rights reserved. No part of this book shall be reproduced or transmitted in any form or by any means, electronic or mechanical, including photocopying, recording, or by an information retrieval system, without written permission from the publisher.

First Printing 1984

Library of Congress Cataloging in Publication Data

Main entry under title:

The American workforce.

(The ITT key issues lecture series)
1. Unemployment, Structural—United States—Addresses, essays, lectures. 2. Manpower policy—United States—Addresses, essays, lectures. 3. Labor supply—United States—Addresses, essays, lectures. I. Ullrich, Robert A. II. Series.
HD5708.47.U6A44 1984   331.12'0973   84-21635
ISBN 0-86569-125-8

Printed in the United States of America.

Contents

RALPH OWEN

1905–1983

This volume is affectionately dedicated to the memory of Ralph Owen, distinguished businessman and generous benefactor of the Owen Graduate School of Management at Vanderbilt University.

Ralph Owen, a native of Hartsville, Tennessee, graduated from Vanderbilt in 1928 and was a star on both the football and the baseball teams. Indeed, he might well have become a professional athlete, had his father not disapproved.

In 1930, Mr. Owen and four other Vanderbilt graduates founded Equitable Securities Company, a small municipal bond house. Unlike many of its competitors, Equitable itself bought and held securities, and many of those investments later paid off handsomely. In 1949 and 1950, Equitable purchased controlling interest in what is now the American Express Company. That investment made Equitable the second largest investment banking house in the country. In 1952, Mr. Owen became Equitable's president, a position he held until his retirement in 1970.

Mr. Owen was Chairman of American Express Company from 1960 to 1968. He served on the board of directors of the American Express Company and on many other corporate boards.

During World War II, he was manager of the Tennessee Region of the Victory Fund for the United States Treasury.

At Vanderbilt, Mr. Owen was a member of the Board of Trust from 1960 on, and he served as vice-chairman of its Executive Committee. He was a Life Associate of the Owen Graduate School of Management and a member of the Chancellor's Council, and he was elected to honorary membership in Beta Gamma Sigma.

When Mr. Owen died in November 1983, he left behind an outstanding record of accomplishment in both business and philanthropy.

October 29, 1984

Samuel B. Richmond, Dean
Owen Graduate School of Management
Vanderbilt University

Preface

Robert A. Ullrich
Professor of Management
Owen Graduate School of Management
Vanderbilt University

The following lectures were presented during the months that spanned the most severe bout of unemployment this nation has experienced since the Great Depression. Nonetheless, the melancholy pall that widespread unemployment cast upon our spirits was lifted briefly as these lectures portrayed the better times ahead that were taking shape from structural characteristics of the then faltering economy.

For example, Michael Wachter argued that the aging of the oversized baby boom will yield a bumper crop of mature, skilled workers that will lead to lower structural unemployment rates and growth in real wages and productivity. The accompanying shortage of young, unskilled workers will drive up their wages, as well. Moreover, robots and related technological innovations have appeared just in time, as it were, to augment the declining pool of unskilled workers, rather than to compete with them for jobs.

Our present concerns with alien workers and illegal immigration, moreover, should be ameliorated, according to Michael Piore, as higher wages attract more American nationals to jobs now left to aliens or as they enable temporary workers to meet their targeted earnings more rapidly and return home before they develop attachments to the United States.

In observing the continued growth of the service sector of the economy, Eli Ginzberg identified a set of national problems that

ix

will be our agenda for the remainder of the decade. A service economy depends on constant additions to the pool of knowledge, which serve as the foundations for new industries, and on a well-educated workforce. Yet, we can expect no major improvements in the quality of the workforce, since the majority of young people today graduate from high school and a large proportion of them go on to college. Ginzberg advocates the creation of new federal training and job programs to help the sizable minority of young people who drop out of school and, consequently, are ill-equipped to compete successfully in the labor market.

Joe Wyatt, however, was less sanguine. He argued that the demands of the emerging "technological society" on our educational institutions will be in excess of those to which those institutions, in their present form, can respond effectively. We are losing faculty to industry and not attracting students in sufficient numbers to technical and scientific fields, even as we observe an alarming decline in student achievement test scores in mathematics and science in the secondary schools.

The Federal Government's ability to intervene successfully in this situation is in doubt. On the one hand, George Johnson argued that it may be impossible within our present political system to design, implement, and administer employment and training programs that help those who need help. Ivar Berg, on the other hand, questioned the bases upon which our analyses and prescriptions have been made in the past and concluded; "We should call moratoria on claims: (1) that there is, at any given moment, *an* equilibrium unemployment rate . . . and (2) that, therefore, we must eschew aggregate demand policies targeted on the production of additional job opportunities in the so-called private sector."

I am deeply grateful to my friend and colleague of long standing, T. Aldrich Finegan of Vanderbilt's Department of Economics and Business Administration, for his enthusiastic support and thoughtful counsel throughout this lecture series, and hereby acknowledge that debt of gratitude.

Foreword

Rand V. Araskog
Chairman, President and Chief Executive
ITT Corporation

Unemployment might well be the subdominant issue overshadowing the American work place for the remainder of this decade. The aftershocks of an unemployment rate that stubbornly hovered near the 10 percent mark for a year and layoffs that spread deep into white-collar staffs were not merely byproducts of another economic recession.

We are experiencing fundamental changes in technology that pose challenges of historic dimensions to our labor force. And, as never before, the underlying implications must be thoroughly understood if we are to make intelligent choices and disciplined responses necessary to shape a progressive future.

Can the private sector continue generating the 3.2 million *new* jobs that will be needed to reduce our joblessness back to the 6.5 percent norm? Will "job sharing" and increased leisure that induce early retirement place a further burden on the social security system? Should America's overemphasis on education as the means for attaining material well-being and social mobility be re-evaluated?

These six lectures explore the major themes with depth and clarity. However, I think the crucial question is neither technical nor economic. It is, "Do we have the wisdom and capacity to meet the demands of structural change through long-range decisions and actions—or will we succumb to the expediency of the present to solve these problems?"

I agree with Professor Eli Ginzberg of Columbia University in Chapter 5, that the job at hand is not reindustrialization but rather the *revitalization* of our economy. We had become preoccupied with manufacturing, while it was services that have been driving our economy. He traces how the whole spectrum of services—banking, accounting, legal services, management consulting, insurance, and advertising—had produced a net export of $30 billion by 1980 to help our international balance of trade.

It is fitting that this volume be dedicated to the late Ralph Owen, an outstanding businessman of unyielding integrity. As one of the founders of Equitable Securities Company, which purchased controlling interest in what is now the American Express Company in 1950, and later as chairman of the board of American Express from 1960 to 1968, he made pioneer contributions in expanding this international service organization which, like ITT, employs many nationals in its overseas offices.

We at ITT are pleased to have supported this timely and thought-provoking series at Vanderbilt's Owen Graduate School of Management. This book will receive the wide distribution that it deserves.

ONE

Unemployment in the American Economy: Types, Causes, and Outlooks for the 1980's

Michael L. Wachter
Professor of Economics and Management
University of Pennsylvania

Michael L. Wachter currently is Professor of Economics and Management at the University of Pennsylvania and has been on that faculty since 1969. He received his B.S. from Cornell University and his M.A. and Ph.D. from Harvard University. In the past few years he has received grants from the National Science Foundation, the National Institutes of Health, the General Electric Foundation, and the Twentieth Century Fund. He has served as a consultant to the Joint Economic Committee, the Department of Labor, and the Council of Economic Advisors and as a commissioner on the Minimum Wage Study Commission. He currently is a member of the National Council on Employment Policy and a senior advisor to the Brookings panel on economic activity.

He is the author of numerous articles on inflation, unemployment, industry wage and price determination, productivity, labor force behavior, and the institutional framework of the product and labor markets. He currently is completing a book on unemployment for the Twentieth Century Fund and co-editing a book entitled Removing Obstacles to Economic Growth.

Note: The research underlying this paper was supported by grants from the General Electric Foundation and the National Institutes of Health.

1

Introduction

In analyzing the nature and causes of unemployment as well as the future outlook, three causal factors appear to be dominant. These elements include the severe decline in business activity that began in 1981 and led to a peak unemployment rate over 10 percent, the underlying demographic features of the labor market, and the threats and promises posed by technological innovation and international trade.

In the short run, fluctuations in the demand for labor that are associated with the business cycle tend to dominate the unemployment picture. In the early 1980's, the influence of the business cycle has been decidedly negative. Once the economy recovers from the current recession, however, unemployment will decline to its equilibrium rate of 6 to 6.5 percent and job creation will not be a problem.

Over the longer run, swings in aggregate demand tend to balance out so that supply forces control the trend in unemployment rates. From the current perspective, the aging of the baby boom is likely to be the single most important event influencing unemployment over the next decade. This demographic change should lead to an increasingly skilled labor force and a significant decline in the equilibrium unemployment rate. A greatly diminished growth rate of the overall labor force, due to the coming of age of the baby bust cohort, should lead to an improvement in the relative wage of unskilled workers. Dealing with the change from excess supply to relative shortages in the less-skilled labor market will be a major challenge and will influence diverse issues that range from immigration and the old voluntary armed forces to social security.

This underlying trend in the labor supply should hasten and in some cases cause the adoption of high technology production processes. In this context the threat of worker displacement due to technological change seems remote. Rather, a quickening of technological innovation and an increase in investment are critical to the growth rate of real wages.

CYCLICAL UNEMPLOYMENT

The Current Downturn in Business Activity

The high unemployment rates of 1981–82 are a cyclical crea-ture, a result of the sharpest recession of the past four decades. The severity of the problem has generated considerable debate over the causes of the downturn. There is a consensus that the immediate cause was a tightening of monetary policy, which led to a reduction of money supply growth rates. In a more general context, the downturn was an unfortunate, but almost certainly inescapable, byproduct of the anti-inflation battle. Coming after a decade of negligible real growth, which was due, in part, to the oil price shocks, inadequate investment, and crowding-out of private sector growth by government deficit, the economic downturn, thus, combined both secular and cyclical elements.

Policymakers brought into office in 1980 or responding to the results of the 1980 election were determined to do battle with inflation and big government, both of which they viewed as damaging to the long-run economic growth of the economy. President Reagan stated in the 1982 Economic Report of the President that: "The combination of . . . ever higher rates of inflation and ever greater intrusion by the Federal Government into the nation's economic life—have played a major part in the fundamental deterioration in the performance of the economy" (p. 4).

Guided by these twin policy goals, the Federal Reserve began to decelerate money supply growth, and the Administration and Congress moved to control federal expenditure programs. Orig-inally, it was hoped that the resulting program (Reaganomics) would yield increasing growth rates and lower inflation. During 1981, a group of economists in the Reagan Administration, the hard-core supply siders, argued that tax cuts and expenditure cuts would allow both targets to be reached. When it became clear, however, that these two goals were mutually exclusive in the short run, the Administration and the Federal Reserve made the anti-inflation goal paramount. As a consequence, restrictive monetary policy was employed, and the economic downturn developed.

This suggests that, although the recession was not a planned event, the risks inherent in the policy course that was adopted were all on the downside. The paramount goal remained disinflation. Although it was hoped that unemployment would not increase, when that eventually occurred, the Federal Reserve and the Administration persevered. That adherence to anti-inflation goals in the face of a developing downturn broke a post-Depression tradition of shifting policy direction at the first signs of a recession.

The inability of economic policy to "fine-tune" the economy has become widely accepted. The general direction of the economy can be strongly influenced by policy, but only with a large standard deviation. The depth of the present downturn was not anticipated. Early in 1982, private business as well as government forecasters were predicting an upturn in late 1982, with a peak in the unemployment rate of approximately 8 to 8.5 percent.*

Inflation-Unemployment Trade-Off: Can Disinflation Occur Without Rising Unemployment?

The positive result from the recession has been the reduced rate of inflation. Although policymakers prefer not to link the two, they are linked. Moreover, the rapidity of the drop in inflation resulted from the severity of the economic decline. The question of whether disinflation inevitably necessitates a recession has received considerable attention among researchers. The traditional view, based on a short-run downward sloping Phillips curve, has indicated that a reduction in the inflation rate would require unemployment to rise above its equilibrium, or full employment, rate. Periods of economic slack place downward pressure on wages and prices, so that inflationary expectations are not realized.

Throughout the 1970's, business plans and union wage settlements were based on the expectation of moderate inflation rates. Those forecasts tended to be too low. Food and fuel shocks, coupled with a commitment to an optimistic assessment of full

---

* During 1982, the unemployment rate peaked at 10.7 percent.

employment, generated increasing inflation. After a prolonged period of underestimating future inflation rates, individuals began to believe that inflation rates would remain high or even continue rising; that is, that the Administration and Federal Reserve would not enforce an anti-inflation policy.

Hence, when policymakers stayed with their restrictive policies, inflationary expectations proved to be too high. The result was that business plans, union wage settlements, and prices, which were based on continually rising inflation, were out of alignment. The sharp drop in aggregate demand and the rise in unemployment were, thus, both caused and affected by the unrealized inflationary expectations.

Recently, some researchers have argued that downturns in economic activity may not be required to reduce inflation. Robert Barro, for example, divides monetary policy into two components—anticipated and unanticipated changes in money supply growth. He claims that it is the latter, the unanticipated actions of the Federal Reserve, that generates unemployment. Past recessions, according to this view, have resulted from unexpected contractionary shifts in monetary policy.

The source of the problem, according to this school of thought, is discretionary monetary policy. Discretionary, countercyclical shifts in monetary policy are, by nature, unanticipated and, hence, contain a surprise element. Since the private sector does not anticipate change, it is forced into a credit crunch when monetary policy is tight. A well-announced and gradual deceleration of the money supply growth, however, might allow the private sector to adjust its credit demands so as to avoid the sharp rise in short-term interest rates and/or credit shortages that are associated with the onset of business downturns.

Unfortunately, there are overwhelming difficulties in implementing this type of policy. First, how can the Federal Reserve make announcements that are believable and understandable? Since most individuals base their expectations on past developments, it is generally assumed that the Federal Reserve will not persevere. In this case, even a pre-announced, gradual deceleration of the money supply, if maintained, would come as a surprise. In addition, a new administration in 1984 or a shift in emphasis by the current one would force the central bank to abandon certain targets. Although the Federal Reserve is independent, it has to be somewhat sensitive to pressure exerted by Congress or the President simply in order to maintain some degree of freedom of action. Hence, even a strong and believable commitment by current policymakers cannot be trusted, if for no other reason than that policymakers can be changed.

Research on the political business cycle adds further emphasis to the instability in policy. Findings suggest that voters are strongly influenced not only by the magnitude of unemployment rates and national incomes but also by their direction of change at the time of an election. The result has been that most administrations have pursued tight policies during their first two years in office and expansionary policies during years three and four. Even a committed anti-inflation regime might be convinced that short-run compromises are necessary in order to ensure the continuation of the anti-inflation policies in the long run. Hence, to capture the middle ground from the opposing party, policy shifts may be geared to the election rather than to the business cycle.

Finally, there is the problem of deciding which monetary policy will translate into near full employment coupled with a slowly decelerating inflation rate. Changes in business sentiment, in the structure of financial institutions, and even in the weather (through its effects on agricultural output), among others, all serve to break any purely deterministic link among monetary policy, inflation, and unemployment. Given this random element, a commitment to reducing inflation rates translates into a high risk of recession.

Although it was hoped that the recession would not occur, policymakers did accept a substantial risk that a downturn in economic activity would accompany disinflation. Whether the anti-inflation goals were worth the severity of the resulting downturn and whether a more gradual deceleration of money supply growth and inflation would have caused less discomfort in the long run will be debated for years. *Ex post,* I suspect that even the Federal Reserve and the Reagan Administration would have preferred a slower reduction in inflation than actually occurred. Since the random component cannot be known in advance, policymakers are forced to make *ex ante* policy decisions with uncertain outcomes.

The Next Recovery

Since the downturn in economic activity accounts for approximately 3.5 to 5 percentage points of the current unemployment rate, the next expansion should reduce the unemployment rate back to 6 or 6.5 percent. Although the current downturn has been severe, few developments, if any, point to a permanent increase in unemployment. In fact, as is discussed below, it is likely that the unemployment rate at full employment, or the equilibrium level of unemployment, will trend downward in the near-term future.

How rapidly the economy rebounds depends, in part, on the future course of government policymaking. If the 1984 election does not yield a change in political-economic philosophy, the expansion probably will be cautious, because of the fear of losing painfully achieved gains against inflation. However, economic policy cannot fine-tune the strength and duration of the recovery any more than it could have predicted the severity of the 1981–82 downturn in business activity. Hence, the policymakers' preference for a restrained upswing, that would minimize both the potential of accelerating inflation and a resulting electoral setback in 1984, might not be realized.

Current economic doctrines support limited, discretionary shifts in economic policy. In the 1960's and early 1970's, shifts in policy tended to be frequent, and the policy mix tended to be highly sensitive to political developments. The evidence on the effects of frequent changes in policy direction suggests that they have done more harm than good. If these lessons have been integrated into policy, fewer shifts and less fine-tuning are to be expected. Political sentiment determines the policy approach and, hence, the risks to be taken. A cautious, conservative policy would have an expected outcome of a slow return to 6 to 6.5 percent unemployment that would minimize the likelihood of accelerating inflation. On the other hand, an alternative, more expansionary course, with a rapid return to a 6 percent unemployment rate, would inrease the likelihood of an upturn in the inflation rate.

In setting the course of an employment policy, it is important to distinguish between the cyclical component of unemployment and its noncyclical component. During downturns, plant closings, international trade displacement, and other such factors take on an air of permanence. Confusion over whether a given set of events is self-limiting and cyclical or secular and long-lasting has led to inappropriate policy responses. During the 1970's, there was a tendency to treat cyclical upturns in unemployment as if they required long-term public service employment programs that, in turn, were geared to the incorrect notion that there was a chronic shortage of jobs. These policies tended to have a perverse, pro-cyclical component. In addition, they generated inefficiencies, including the crowding-out of private sector employment. Thus, a secular bias existed that responded to layoffs in the private sector with new jobs in the public sector.

THE SUPPLY-SIDE VIEW OF YOUTH UNEMPLOYMENT

The Increasing Equilibrium Rate of Unemployment

A discussion of the employment and unemployment outlook for the next several years must take cognizance of both the stage of the business cycle and the underlying labor supply developments. The nature of the recovery in business activity is likely to be the dominant factor in the labor market. An optimistic outcome would be a return to an unemployment rate of approximately 6 percent without accelerating inflation.

The success of economic policy in achieving this outcome depends, in part, on the acceptance of the limitations of discretionary monetary and fiscal policies. Of particular relevance is the overly optimistic full-employment goal pursued by the government over the past two decades. Monetary and fiscal policies have been pushed too far in pursuit of 4 percent unemployment rates. The result has been accelerating inflation.

Expansionary monetary and fiscal policies can cure cyclical unemployment, once the economy has reached what is called the "equilibrium" unemployment rate; however, the cost of further reductions in unemployment is spiraling inflation. The "equilibrium" rate of unemployment is the minimum unemployment rate that is compatible with a stable rate of inflation. When unemployment is below the equilibrium rate, inflation increases as firms bid wages higher to attract workers. When unemployment is above the equilibrium rate, the rate of inflation subsides.

Thus, zero cyclical unemployment exists when the actual unemployment rate is equal to the equilibrium rate. When the economy is at its equilibrium unemployment, any remaining unemployment cannot be due to a shortage of jobs.

There has been a secular rise in the unemployment rates across cyclical peaks since the 1960's. Hence, an unemployment rate of 3.5 percent in 1968 was followed by a 4.9 percent rate in the peak year of 1973 and a 5.8 percent rate in 1979. I argue that this rise in unemployment rates, across peaks in business activity, has not been due to a chronic shortfall in jobs or aggregate demand. Rather, the rise in the equilibrium unemployment rate has been due to labor supply forces and, in particular, to demographic factors. Thus, a secular rise in the equilibrium rate of unemployment has necessitated a higher level of unemployment at every stage in the business cycle. The equilibrium unemployment rate was approximately 4.0 percent in the full employment year of 1955, but it increased to the range of 5.8 and 6.4 percent during the last business cycle in 1979. My estimates of the equilibrium unemployment rate are presented in Table 1. Two separate series are presented that include both optimistic and pessimistic views of how the equilibrium rate has changed. Note that the equilibrium rate, although still high, probably has begun to decline. The 1981–82 upsurge in unemployment has been a cyclical phenomenon.

Of particular importance in the secular trend underlying the equilibrium unemployment rate is the demographic shift toward younger and female workers. Young male and female workers have been increasing as a percentage of the labor force as a direct consequence of the baby boom of the late 1950's. For young male workers, labor force participation rates have increased somewhat, so that the increase in their relative population size translates directly into an increase in their relative percentage in the labor force. For young females, including those age 16 through 34, rapidly increasing participation rates have resulted in a dramatic increase in labor force growth. Whereas workers in the age group 16 to 24 accounted for 16.7 percent of labor force in 1960, they now constitute approximately 25 percent. Of the increase in the

Table 1
Unemployment, Actual and Equilibrium Rates

Year	Actual	U^*_1	U^*_2
1954	5.5	3.8	4.2
1955	4.4	3.8	4.2
1956	4.1	3.9	4.3
1957	4.3	3.9	4.7
1958	6.8	3.9	4.9
1959	5.5	4.0	5.0
1960	5.5	4.2	5.1
1961	6.7	4.2	5.2
1962	5.5	4.2	5.3
1963	5.7	4.4	5.4
1964	5.2	4.6	5.7
1965	4.5	4.8	5.1
1966	3.8	4.9	4.5
1967	3.8	5.0	4.6
1968	3.6	5.0	4.6
1969	3.5	5.2	4.8
1970	4.9	5.3	5.2
1971	5.9	5.5	6.2
1972	5.6	5.7	6.6
1973	4.9	5.8	7.0
1974	5.6	5.8	6.8
1975	8.5	5.8	6.4
1976	7.7	5.9	6.4
1977	7.0	5.9	6.4
1978	6.0	5.9	6.5
1979	5.8	5.8	6.4
1980	7.1	5.7	6.3
1981	7.6	5.6	6.2

Source: The equilibrium unemployment series were constructed by the author. See also Michael L. Wachter, "The Changing Cyclical Responsiveness of Wage Inflation Over the Postwar Period," *Brookings Papers on Economic Activity,* vol. 1 (1976), pp. 115–159; and Jeffrey M. Perloff and Michael L. Wachter, "A Production Function-Nonaccelerating Inflation Approach to Potential Output: Is Measured Potential Output Too High?" in K. Brunner and A. H. Meltzer, eds., *Carnegie-Rochester Conference Series on Public Policy,* vol. 10 (1979), pp. 113–163, for a description of the methodology.

U^*_1 : An optimistic projection of equilibrium unemployment.
U^*_2 : A middle-ground projection of equilibrium unemployment (including the effect of oil price shocks).

equilibrium unemployment rate over the past two decades, a full percentage point is due to the changing composition of the labor force.

Imperfect Substitution

Why does it make a difference if the supply of young workers is increasing rapidly? The explanation is based on the fact that young workers are imperfect substitutes for older, more experienced workers. This distinction is fundamental. Whereas older workers have a high degree of job attachment and accumulated job-specific knowledge, younger workers have little job-specific knowledge and many have not made a career decision.

The imperfect substitution argument is rooted in the technology and cost functions of firms. The nature of the machinery and the complexity of the job, among other factors, dictate the type of workers who will be most productive and least costly on that job. Some jobs call for considerable skills that are specific to the firm and require workers who have strong job attachments. A great number of other jobs require little training or knowledge that is specific to the firm and, hence, can be filled by transient workers, who may want to work only part of the time.

Essentially, youths simply cannot "work anywhere." Rather, they are confined to certain occupations within certain industries where they replace, or are used in place of, capital equipment. These types of jobs are prevalent in the service and retail sectors, where youths work with little supervision and capital equipment.

Since young workers tend to be inexperienced and, hence, cannot replace older workers who are better trained to perform specific tasks, any shift in the relative supply of young versus older workers in relation to the normal demand for the two types of workers will alter the wages, employment conditions, and upward mobility of the two groups. In particular, when younger workers are in relatively abundant supply compared with older workers, their wages, employment conditions, and upward mobility will be unfavorably affected.

Social Welfare Programs

A large increase in the flow of young workers into a competitive labor market need not create a structural unemployment problem. (Because of the compositional shift, U^* might increase to 5 percent, but it need not go above that level.) Its major impact should be on relative wages. In particular, since younger and older workers are imperfect substitutes for each other, an overcrowded youth cohort should depress the relative wages of young workers. For example, whereas 20- to 24-year-old males earned almost three-fourths of what 45- to 51-year-old male workers earned in 1955, they earned only slightly more than half as much as prime-age males after 1975. This is shown in Table 2.

However, it appears that the decline in relative wages was not sufficient to prevent the rise in structural unemployment. Do labor markets, especially for unskilled workers, have institutional features that encourage unemployment? Of potential importance are the minimum wage, public assistance, and other transfer programs for the poor. These programs have changed dramatically since the 1960's.

For minimum wages, the increase has been dramatic but somewhat indirect, operating through an increase in the coverage of minimum wages rather than the minimum wage level itself. The mandated minimum wage as a percentage of the wage in manufacturing has not increased since 1939. Basically, in setting the minimum wage, the unannounced but obvious intent of Congress has been to fix the minimum wage at approximately 50 percent of the manufacturing wage.

Until the 1960's, however, most low wage sectors of the econ-

Table 2
Relative Income for Males by Age[a]

| Year | 14 to 19[b] | Income of Males of Each Age Group Divided by Income of Males Age 45 to 54 | | | | |
		20 to 24	25 to 34	35 to 44	45 to 54	55 to 64
1955	.4084	.7331	.9593	1.0049	1.0	.8816
1960	.3477	.6897	.9598	1.0403	1.0	.8945
1965	.4495	.6882	.9557	1.0524	1.0	.9196
1970	.3977	.6701	.9189	1.0329	1.0	.9134
1975	.3820	.5754	.8628	.9947	1.0	.9126
1979	.3674	.5610	.8221	.9807	1.0	.9498

Source: The income data are from United States Bureau of the Census, Current Population Reports, Series P-60, *Income of Families and Persons in the United States,* various issues.

[a]The relative income data are calculated by dividing the age-sex specific income by that of males age 45 to 54. The year-round, full-time worker earnings are used.

[b]The age group has been changed to 15–19 year-olds.

omy, such as the service and retail sectors, were not covered by the minimum wage legislation. The major industries that hired numerous workers at low wages could obtain exemptions from the minimum wage laws by arguing before Congress that significant unemployment would result if they were forced to pay the minimum. The result was a policy exempting most of those workers and industries that might have been affected by minimum wages. In many respects, the United States did not have an operational minimum wage policy until the 1960's.

In 1961 and 1967, the Fair Labor Standards Act was amended to extend coverage to the low-wage sectors. For example, the coverage rate prior to 1961 was approximately 53 percent of nonsupervisory workers, but after 1967 it reached 75 percent. Many of the newly covered workers were in the low-wage sectors. An index created especially for youth indicates that their effective coverage has more than doubled since the 1960's.

Changes in other social welfare programs complemented the policy direction exhibited in the minimum wage policy. The eligibility criteria for welfare programs were liberalized and the number of programs was increased during the 1960's and 1970's. For example, the number of families on AFDC increased astronomically from 1.73 percent of United States families to 6.22 percent in 1975. The percentage of individuals in the American population on this welfare program showed a similar jump from 1.66 percent to 5.31 percent.

In addition, the largest growth in welfare has been in income-in-kind transfers, such as food stamps, which do not appear in the Aid to Families with Dependent Children data. Not only has the growth rate in food stamp payments been large, funding for this program has now reached a significant proportion of total welfare payments. Consequently, there has been a significant increase in total welfare payments relative to market wages over the past 10 years.

The "Cost of Being Unemployed"

In analyzing the effects of decreasing market wages for young workers and the increasing levels of minimum wage and welfare programs, it is useful to introduce the notion of the "cost of being unemployed."

That cost would be equal to the total income (in wage payments) that could be received by working compared to the income available from transfer payments. Defined in this fashion, the "cost of being unemployed" was considerably smaller by the end of the 1970's than it was at the beginning of the 1960's. Since the relative "costs of being unemployed" fall as the transfer floor is increased relative to prevailing wages, a trade-off exists, particularly for those workers who can earn only low wages in the labor market. The less the relative cost of not working, the greater the possibility that an individual will search longer for a job and/or draw welfare payments.

It is likely that the explicit minimum wage law and welfare policies strongly support each other in establishing an effective minimum wage. Whereas the minimum wage creates a floor for employers on the demand side of the labor market, the welfare program sets a floor for potential employees on the supply side of the market. Legislation for these two sets of programs tends to move together; liberalized relative to market wages between 1960 and 1975, steady between 1975 and 1980, and declining after 1980.

Viewed in this fashion, the "cost of being unemployed"—that is, the social or explicit minimum wage relative to overall market wages—declined between 1960 and 1975. In addition, since the youth wage fell relative to the adult wage during that period, the "cost of being unemployed" declined significantly for youth.

Characteristics of Structural Unemployment

In essence, then, the model suggested here predicts that the "cost of being unemployed" is relevant to the number of people who will be unemployed when the economy is close to its full employment level. To appreciate this factor, several crucial features of the work force and the unemployment pool when the economy is close to its equilibrium unemployment rate must be noted.

1. In a year such as 1979, when the unemployment rate of 5.8 percent was close to the equilibrium level, most of those who were unemployed entered the unemployment pool because of worker-initiated actions; a disproportionate number were unskilled, young workers.

In 1979, for example, approximately 50 percent of the unemployment was accounted for by workers in the 16 to 24 age group. Three of the lowest-skilled occupational categories (service workers, nonfarm laborers, and operatives) accounted for 50 percent of the unemployment. On the other hand, these three categories included only 30 percent of total employment. Layoffs, the cause of unemployment typically associated with recessions and inadequate demand, accounted for only 14 percent of the unemployment pool in 1979. Unemployment spells initiated by actions of the workers (quits, re-entrants, and new entrants) accounted for almost 60 percent of the total unemployment. For teenagers, only 5.4 percent of the unemployed were on layoff status and 80 percent were either re-entrants, new entrants, or job leavers.

2. The duration of unemployment is extremely short. In 1979, 48 percent of the unemployed had been unemployed for less than five weeks, and 80 percent had been unemployed for less than 14 weeks. The short duration of unemployment actually was more pronounced for youth than for adults, probably reflecting the greater unemployment compensation coverage of adult workers.

3. The single-wage-earner family is a sharply reduced component of the labor force. In 1981, only 31 percent of the families in the United States had a single wage earner in the previous 12 months, 13 percent had zero wage earners, and 56 percent had two or more wage earners.

4. The growth in the two-wage-earner family has created an important distinction between the low-wage worker and the worker from a low-income family. In 1979, only one out of seven labor force participants who experienced unemployment during the year resided in a poor family. Over one-half of the unemployed resided in families with incomes above $15,000, which is just below the median family income level.

To summarize, when the economy is close to its equilibrium unemployment level of 6 percent, the unemployment pool has a number of important characteristics. The great bulk of the unemployed are young workers age 16 to 24 and workers with low skill levels. There are few prime-age skilled workers in the unemployment pool. Moreover, workers are unemployed largely because of actions that they have, at least in part, initiated. Only a small minority of workers are on layoff status, which is the type of unemployment normally associated with cyclical fluctuations. Finally, few of the unemployed are in poverty and, indeed, somewhat less than one-half come from families with above average income.

LABOR SUPPLY AND
UNEMPLOYMENT PROJECTIONS

Population Factors

Developments in the youth labor market are crucial to the trend in structural unemployment. This is due to the fact that youths have a much higher incidence of unemployment than do adults. When the economy is close to its equilibrium unemployment rate, as in 1979, 50 percent of the unemployed are age 16 to 24. As the baby bust cohort begins to replace the baby boom cohort in the youth labor market, the percentage of the labor market that is age 16 to 24 will decline dramatically from 23.5 to 17.1 percent by 1990 (see Table 3). This 8.4 percentage decline corresponds to an absolute decline of 3.6 million youth workers. Since the youth labor market increased by 6.8 million workers during the 1970's, this demographic swing represents an unprecedented shift of 10.4 million workers. Moreover, the number of youth in the labor force will continue to decline through the 1980's.

On the other hand, the percentage of workers age 25 to 44 will increase by over 18 million in the 1980's. Whereas 39.2 percent of the population was age 25 to 44 in 1975, representation of that age cohort will grow to 54.6 percent by 1990.

An important result of this shift in the composition of the labor force is that there will be fewer individuals in the high-unemployment age groups and many more individuals in their prime-age, stable working period. This change alone should lead to a drop of 1 percentage point in the aggregate unemployment rate by 1990.

An Increased "Cost of Being Unemployed"

The supply outlook is even more favorable than that suggested above. As the size of the youth population declines, overcrowding in that labor market should diminish and real wages should increase. The potential of increased growth rates of real wages is the major gain associated with the changing demographic profile of the country.

Since youth and the unskilled are closest to the minimum wage, their wage rates are key determinants of the "cost of being unemployed." As market wages for the least-skilled workers increase, the minimum wage will have less of a detrimental effect on employment opportunities. Fewer workers will be priced out of jobs. Moreover, as market wages increase, AFDC payments, food stamps, subsidized housing, and the like will become relatively less attractive. In general, increases in market wages are paralleled by increases in the "cost of being unemployed."

Table 3
Relative Civilian Labor Force* (1965 to 2000)

Age	1965	1970	1975	1980
16-19	7.9	8.8	9.5	8.8
20-24	11.1	12.8	14.5	14.7
25-34	19.1	20.6	21.1	26.9
35-44	22.6	19.9	18.1	19.3
45-54	21.2	20.5	18.5	16.2
55-64	13.9	13.6	12.1	11.2
65+	4.2	3.9	3.2	2.9
Total	100.0	100.0	100.0	100.0

Age	1985	1990	1995	2000
16-19	7.3	6.3	5.6	6.0
20-24	13.2	10.8	9.6	8.9
25-34	28.5	28.1	25.9	22.9
34-44	22.7	26.5	27.1	26.1
45-54	14.8	15.5	19.1	22.6
55-64	10.7	10.0	9.9	10.8
65+	2.8	2.9	2.9	2.8
Total	100.0	100.0	100.0	100.0

Source: Based on calculations by the author. See Michael L. Wachter, "The Economic Challenges Posed by Demographic Changes," in *Work Decisions in the 1980s* (Boston: Auburn House, 1982), pp. 35-75.

*Percent of the civilian labor force by age group.

Not only is the market wage increasing, the value of transfer payments is decreasing as well. A component of President Reagan's program and Congressional expenditure bills indicate a trimming of the growth of social welfare expenditures. This means that eligibility is being tightened, most directly affecting individuals who can work. In some cases, programs, such as the food stamps program, are being substantially reduced in real and even nominal terms. Although these changes are likely to have beneficial macroeconomic effects on unemployment rates, they are likely to generate significant costs for the low-income population.

Minimum wages also are becoming less of a factor. In 1978, the FLSA was amended to provide increases in the minimum wage effective the first of January in 1979, 1980, and 1981. That act has not been amended again, so the minimum wage has not changed since January 1, 1981. At the current time, it appears that the minimum wage freeze will remain in effect at least through 1984, with the result that the relative level of the minimum wage will decline dramatically as prices and wages continue to rise.

Thus, it appears that both the new political mood, that has the effect of reducing welfare benefits, and changing demographics will continue to increase substantially the "cost of being unemployed" by increasing market wages and decreasing the number of youth. As that key determinant of unemployment increases during the 1980's, breaking two decades of downward movement, the equilibrium unemployment rate will decrease further. It is very difficult to quantify this effect and impossible to predict how it might change after the 1984 election. However, a very rough approximation suggests that the current changes in legislation, if retained, could interact with the demographics to push the equilibrium unemployment rate down by another 0.75 points over the next decade.

Labor Demand Projections

Having outlined what I view to be the key labor supply developments of the 1980's, it is useful to compare them with other projections that deal mostly with the demand for workers. It is frequently argued that the increasing adoption of computers in many sectors of the economy will create a lopsided demand for highly skilled workers who are trained to use that technology efficiently. At the same time, the addition of industrial robots and other labor-saving devices will decrease the demand for less skilled, blue-collar workers. The resulting scenario is that employment of highly skilled workers will increase dramatically, causing a shortage of those workers, while the demand for lower-skilled individuals will slacken, causing unemployment.

I would argue that such forecasts of increasing employment of skilled workers are correct, but not for the reasons suggested above. The moving force will not be labor-saving technological change; rather, it will be the dramatically increasing supply of skilled workers during the 1980's. Prime-age workers will find jobs and, hence, the employment of highly skilled workers will increase because there will be so many more of them. In the market for less-skilled labor and, hence, in the youth market, the labor supply will decline. Thus, the relative employment levels of less-skilled workers will decrease, but largely because there will be so few of them.

In other words, the evolving *employment* pattern predicted by the "high-tech" argument may occur, but it will be driven by demographic, supply-side factors. Absent the supply developments, the adoption of the new technologies would be slowed because of cost considerations. These technologies tend to require relatively skilled or, more specifically, reliable operators—in part because the equipment with which they work is expensive. If the relative wages of these individuals were high, reflecting a supply shortage, any increase in demand for them would be dampened by further increases in their relative wage. However, this will not be the case. In the 1980's, the baby boom will be in the prime-age group, providing a surfeit of workers with high job attachment and reliability. The increase in their supply would, thus, cause a reduction in their relative wages, were it not for induced changes in technologies.

Hence, with respect to employment, both supply and demand stories predict similar developments. They differ, however, with respect to unemployment, the location of worker shortages, and upward pressure on wages. My argument is that a surplus, rather than a shortage, of highly skilled workers will facilitate the adoption of high technology capital. The shortage will be for entry level, less-skilled workers. This being the case, relative wages for young workers will begin to increase in the 1980's, restoring some of the relative wage loss of the 1960's and 1970's.

In analyzing demand projections, it is necessary to evaluate the potential for successful predictions in this area. Projections of the demand for labor inherently are more difficult to make than predictions of the labor supply. Since the population age 0 to 16 is known at any point in time, the number of people who will be entering the labor market for the first time over the next 10 to 15 years has a large, predetermined component. Moreover, years of education completed and hours of work are relatively stable or slowly changing and, hence, can be projected. Greater uncertainty is attached to the total number of legal and illegal immigrants and to labor force participation rates.

On the demand side, however, there are no hard, predetermined factors comparable to the population figures on the supply side of the market. Presumably, one can always project existing trends, and this, by and large, is the technique adopted by the Bureau of Labor Statistics. But this type of projection cannot be interpreted as having any economic or demographic basis. It is hardly possible to predict, on the basis of *a priori* models or predetermined data, whether the present demand-side trends will continue into the future.

A widely accepted hypothesis in economics is that demand-side factors control the short run, but supply-side factors determine the long run. For example, average hours of work over the next two years will depend heavily on the timing of the economic recovery. Over a longer time horizon, however, demand factors will have to accommodate themselves to the available manpower pool. The high labor cost of attempting to move against the supply trends leads to induced changes in the techniques of production. In the short run, the technology is fixed, but over time it increasingly becomes a variable factor. Profit maximization rules imply that employment will accommodate the abundant and, hence, relatively cheap age-sex-skill labor supply groups.

The dominance of long-run supply factors is overridden only by major technological innovations on the demand side. Exogenous changes in technology will alter the relative wages and attractiveness of different occupations, inducing a supply adjustment. This type of development is atypical. In fact, a close reading of the "high-tech" literature indicates that the anticipated changes are not purely exogenous events. First, international competition and the relatively high labor costs of American production workers are driving the adoption of robots and other, more automated production processes. Second, the available labor supply is favorable to these developments; that is, computers and related technologies are excellent examples of how technology has adapted itself to the available manpower. To understand this phenomenon, one must address a basic puzzle. Is it likely that large-scale adoption of expensive, complicated computer-based facilities will result in a knowledge gap that will leave numerous managers and production workers dumbfounded and unable to use the new equipment? Will management junk its current capital equipment in order to shift to the "best available technology"?

Past evidence related to these types of changes suggests that both questions should be answered negatively. Although it is still the case that most young people are not sophisticated in terms of computer usage, computers have learned to work with people as much as people have learned to work with computers; that is, computers and people have learned to accommodate each other.

Computers have become less expensive, less bulky, and much easier to use. Learning by doing is no longer astronomically expensive as it was in the 1960's, when the novice had limited practice time because of the high cost of using (experimenting on) mainframe computers. Microprocessors have brought the computer out of the isolated computer center and into the offices of managers. In addition, hardware changes and the proliferation of software packages have made computer use sufficiently simple that any average person with some interest can learn the techniques in a matter of weeks. It is simply too expensive to adopt technologies that the tenured labor force cannot use effectively.

The story of computers is part of an ongoing historical saga in which the threat of technological change is associated with widescale labor displacement and unemployment. Looking back over time, one can find demand projections for every decade that suggested wholesale unemployment of less-skilled workers. This has never occurred, however—at least not as a result of technology.

The answer to the second question is also negative. It is a well-established empirical fact that, although the best available technology may govern net new investment in capital, the average capital stock is adjusted slowly. Indeed, heralded new technologies such as robotics, biogenetics, solar energy, to name just a few recent examples, often are not cost effective compared to established capital. Even new additions to the capital stock may adopt, for example, conventional machine tools for quite some time, because the new methods are not available for widespread usage. In addition, even as the new methods become available, interest costs, production disruptions that result from the adoption of new technologies, new labor training costs, severance pay (if mandated), and the like will further slow the diffusion process.

The 1970's provide an illustration of the slow diffusion of new technologies. The computer, for example, was available in the 1960's, as were sophisticated machine tools (the early robots). Yet, the massive gains in employment in the 1970's occurred in the less skilled retail and service sectors. The initial entry of the baby boom into the youth labor market and the increasing participation rate of young females dominated the evolving employment pattern. This supply factor caused relative wages to change and this *induced* a change in the demand for labor in favor of less-skilled workers.

I believe that the same type of causation will dominate the 1980's; in the next decade, the aging of the baby boom population will encourage and, indeed, cause the adoption of computers, robots, and other high technology capital goods. Indeed, these induced changes on the demand side will be necessary if the baby boom and bust cohorts are to be successfully integrated into the labor market. High technology capital goods will continue to shrink relative employment among blue-collar workers, and computers will continue to contribute to the explosive growth in information management in the white-collar sectors. In these cases, technology will continue to adapt to user capabilities, the relative labor cost, and the availability of highly skilled workers.

The result should be minimal disruption of established work forces. Paralleling our experience of the past two decades, manufacturing employment probably will not grow. However, the slow diffusion process should require only attrition, rather than layoffs of workers with long tenure. It will be in areas where new products are in demand, for both domestic and international markets, that the new technologies will find quickest application.

Given the underlying demographics, increased rather than re-duced rates of diffusion will be beneficial.

Conclusion

Throughout the 1980's, unemployment and employment developments will be affected by two broad factors. Cyclical unemployment will be an important issue due to the severe economic downturn in business activity that began in 1980. Having pursued unrealistic unemployment goals during the 1960's and 1970's, the nation must now confront the problem posed by high rates of inflation at high unemployment rates. 1981–82 have proved that disinflation will be costly.

An important issue is whether policymakers adopt realistic goals for unemployment and growth. This will determine whether the anti-inflation gains prove to be permanent or temporary. I have argued that the over-optimistic full employment and potential output targets of the late 1960's and 1970's bear a responsibility for the economy's current unfavorable trade-off between unemployment and inflation. This situation can be improved if we avoid overheating the economy. Unfortunately, there is uncertainty as to the current equilibrium unemployment rates. Moreover, they continue to change each year. This means that we must be prepared to tolerate a margin of error and accept the cost of somewhat higher unemployment than would be needed in a world with economic certainty.

The current, short-run negatives associated with the cyclical factors should be distinguished from the long-run positives associated with the demographic, labor supply factors. The aging of the oversized baby boom cohort should yield a trend toward lower equilibrium unemployment rates throughout the 1980's. In addition, the growth in the prime-age work force should provide for growth in real wages and productivity.

In this supply context, the issue of computer-based technological change appears to be beneficial and necessary if the supply potential is to be realized. The demographic, labor supply developments translate into large increases in the number of workers, age 25 to 44, during the 1980's. Those individuals tend to have above-average job attachment, reliability, and job-specific training. With some additional training, this oversized cohort can efficiently use the emerging technological processes.

Due primarily to labor supply availability and only secondarily to technology, the employment picture in 1990 should show the most rapid growth in above-average-skilled employment. Unskilled employment actually should decline. The equilibrium unemployment rate should trend downward over the decade. Policy decisions, as well as the unavoidable and unforeseen exogenous shocks, will determine the actual level of unemployment as well as the accompanying inflation rate. Unfortunately, the "correct" policy, in the sense of the one that maximizes real output growth, remains a mystery.

TWO

Employment and Training Programs in the United States: What Do We Know, and Where Should We Go From Here?

George E. Johnson
Professor of Economics and Public Policy
The University of Michigan, Ann Arbor

George E. Johnson is Professor of Economics at the University of Michigan, Ann Arbor, where he has served since 1966. Professor Johnson received his B.S. from Babson College and the M.A. and Ph.D. from the University of California, Berkeley. He also has served as Visiting Research Fellow at the University of Nairobi; Director, Office of Evaluation in the U.S. Department of Labor; Senior Staff Economist on the President's Council of Economic Advisors; and Visiting Research Fellow at the London School of Economics and Political Science.

A labor economist, Professor Johnson has been a frequent contributor to the literature in his field. His research interests have ranged from trade unionism to the academic labor market to labor and employment policies.

Introduction

Employment and training programs provide subsidized jobs and/or training opportunities to selected members of the potential labor force. In a sense, they are the active component of our labor market policy, and, over the past 50 years, have been a response to various perceptions of problems with the free workings of the labor market. At the present time, the prevalent political mood of the country is anti-interventionist. The Reagan Administration has been able to reduce substantially the budgetary resources allocated to employment and training programs, despite the existence of a prolonged spell of severe unemployment. I make no pretenses at being a political (or, for that matter, an *economic*) guru, but it seems safe to predict that the employment and training apparatus will be rebuilt sometime in the relatively near future. Whether this happens in 1985 or 1989 depends on whether the Reagan team is returned for a second term and on the strength of the 1983 economic recovery.

Labor market policy in the United States has taken several turns, as I will demonstrate. We have tried a large number of different programs. Assuming that my prediction of a new set of "programmatic thrusts" in the mid or late 1980's is correct, it is clearly to our benefit to ask what we have learned about such programs. Which previous approaches appear to have been more successful and which ones less successful? What have we learned from our past experience that can be of use in future efforts to formulate policy?

The general answer to these questions is that we have learned a little bit, but not very much—certainly not as much as we should have learned. It is my opinion—and I realize that some economists would disagree—that it will not be possible for an honest, informed advisor to the next President to say that, based on our experience with the labor market programs of the 1960's and 1970's, the funding of programs A, B, and C will have results X, Y, and Z. The reason we learned so little is an interesting story, one to which I will return at several points.

Phases of Employment and Training Policy

To appreciate the problems encountered in attempting to understand these programs, it is useful to put them in a general historical context. First, as I have mentioned, employment and training programs are only the activist part of a national labor market policy. Other programs, some of which appear to be far removed from the domain of the United States Department of Labor, have labor market consequences that overwhelm any possible impacts of employment and training programs. For example, the policies that affect educational funding, to a very great extent, shape the distribution of skills in the aggregate labor force. Military manpower policy has a major short-run impact on the civilian supply of younger workers as well as a longer-term impact on the skill distribution of the labor force. Immigration policy is a very important determinant of the aggregate supply of low-skilled labor.

Federal policies governing social security and transfer payments to the poor influence the age and skill distribution of the aggregate labor force. A progressive Federal income tax system affects the aggregate quantity and skill distribution of the labor force. These programs are administered by, respectively, the Departments of Education, Defense, Justice, Health and Human Services (and to some extent, Agriculture), and the Treasury.

Other, more direct aspects of labor market policy also influence the problems that employment and training programs are designed to alleviate. The Federal minimum wage under the Fair Labor Standards Act of 1938 exists, in part, to discourage the substitution of young and low-skilled workers for high-wage, unionized workers. To the extent that the minimum wage is successful in achieving this objective, there will be large-scale structural unemployment of young workers—a result, by the way, that provided justification for the creation of myriad youth employment programs in the 1970's. Policies that encourage or discourage union growth and power influence the importance and size of the union/nonunion wage differential and, thus, the rate of queue unemployment (i.e., people who remain unemployed in order to search for high-wage, union jobs). Policies (or the lack of same) that address equal pay and affirmative action have had some very subtle influences on the unemployment situation for minorities.

The first phase of the modern experience with employment and training programs began with the Manpower Development and Training Act of 1962. The perceived problem at that time was a mismatch between the supplies of and demands for different types of labor skills. The MDTA provided retraining, relocation, job information, and other remedial services to technologically displaced workers. By the time it was discovered that this perception of the state of the labor market was erroneous, President Johnson's War on Poverty had commenced. Training the unskilled became one of its weapons, and employment and training programs moved into their second phase. The third phase of the development of these programs occurred during the early 1970's, beginning with a slight shift in emphasis from training to federally subsidized employment through local governments under the Emergency Employment Act of 1971. Next, the MDTA programs were decentralized under the Comprehensive Employment and Training Act of 1973, a concept originally called "manpower revenue sharing."

The fourth phase of the development of employment and training programs occurred in the mid-1970's, and was based on the notion that an expansion of public employment (along the lines of the CETA model) could mitigate both cyclical and structural unemployment. By fiscal year 1978, 1.4 million jobs were supported by Federal funds under various titles. The Carter Administration's welfare reform proposal (the Program for Better Jobs and Incomes) included additional jobs in excess of one million, but this proposal was not passed by the Congress. During this time the Humphrey-Hawkins Act, which would have provided a public sector job at "prevailing wages" for every unemployed person, was proposed and widely discussed. This act eventually was passed as the Full Employment and Balanced Growth Act of 1978, but it was entirely symbolic and created employment only for a few economists and typists.

The most recent phase in the modern history of employment and training programs is characterized by their scuttling under the Reagan Administration. The Reagan Administration's scenario describing the operation of the economy holds that federally supported jobs that are targeted toward particular segments of the labor force do not lead to "real" jobs and socially useful production. Rather, the route to a real and lasting betterment of the status of low-income workers is through an increase in the capital stock that is brought about, in turn, by reductions in taxes on asset income and in government spending. In addition, work incentives for the poor have been increased by reducing transfer payments relative to what their levels would have been if Carter had been re-elected. Some training programs remain, but CETA and the employment programs of the 1970's for the most part have been gutted.

Evaluation Evidence

There are several reasons why we know so little about the impact of past employment and training programs. The first is that, because the programs changed so often (more often, actually, than is suggested by the five phases identified above) there was little opportunity to study any program intensively. With training programs, for example, the target clientele changed from the most "job-ready" of the unemployed during the early 1960's to those most disadvantaged in the labor market. If one had attempted to set up an evaluation procedure to determine whether a particular "treatment" had been effective, it would have been nearly impossible to separate out the "participant selection bias" effect from the true programmatic effect on participants' future employment and earnings. This problem obviously was confounded under CETA, for eventually each local area "prime sponsor" determined its own set of programs.

An important criterion of effectiveness that we have attempted to apply to the public employment programs of the 1970's concerns the extent to which local governments used federal subsidies to hire the same number and the same type of workers they would have hired in the absence of those programs. Estimates of this "fiscal substitution effect" have ranged from about 20 to close to 100 percent, with an average estimate of 60 percent. (The average estimate implies that, of each dollar given to local governments to fund employment expansion, 40 cents went for the intended purpose while 60 cents were spent on other activities—for example, purchases of equipment, tax reduction, surplus enhancement, and the like). Partly in response to these estimates, the Department of Labor issued a succession of regulations concerning who could be hired by local governments, at what wage, and for how long. It became increasingly difficult for local governments (except the city of Detroit, which was exempted from such regulations) to use the funds to pay for regular operations. As a result, local governments tended not to use all of their grants in the later period of CETA.

But, what could an evaluator have done to analyze the impact of the CETA program? By 1979, the public employment component of CETA had become very different from what it had been in 1977. Comparisons of post-program labor market successes of participants and nonparticipants would have yielded very different results in 1977 and 1979. No doubt, the 1977 results would have indicated a much greater degree of success than the results for 1979 would have indicated. This does not mean that the PSE program became less efficient during that period. Indeed, there probably was no _real_ program in 1977; there was only a vehicle for inter-governmental transfer payments that permitted the substitution of federal tax collections and deficits for local government tax collections.

It is difficult enough for astronomers and psychologists, respectively, to study the laws of celestial motion and of human behavior, when the underlying phenomena change very slowly. However, if galactic positions and human nature changed radically every three or five years, their tasks would become nearly impossible. Determining whether or not a training program is worth a given amount of public expenditure certainly is less complicated than assessing the validity of the big bang theory or the merits of alternative methods of toilet training, but the instability of such programs makes the evaluation task extremely difficult, nonetheless.

A second reason why our attempts to evaluate the effectiveness of employment and training programs have produced such meager evidence is that it is generally not in any relevant person's interest to gather such evidence. During only one of the five phases identified above (the third, which occurred during the Nixon-Ford years) was evaluation taken at all seriously. During the first two phases, the major impetus was to get legislation passed and the programs funded. To have set up formal, ongoing evaluation processes at the outset of such programs would have had the effect of admitting to serious reservations about the efficacy of the programs themselves. Since the programs were based on such good intentions, anyone in government who had suggested that their efficacy was problematical would have been considered a reactionary at best. Indeed, as it turned out, the only reasonably good data set on the performance of the MDTA programs was collected by virtue of bureaucratic accident.

The consensus concerning the efficacy of MDTA programs was very different during the early 1970's. It was clear, then, that they would not solve all of the country's labor market problems; given their small size, there was no reason to expect that they would. Nonetheless, moderate Republican incumbents of middle management positions in the Labor Department asked the bureaucracy specific questions about the performance of the individual beneficiaries of employment programs. They were told, of course, that very little information on performance was available. In response, resources were allocated to the long-run evaluations of the various programs. Consequently, the period from 1972 to 1976 is now referred to as the "golden age" of evaluation in the employment and training area.

During the late 1970's, with the advent of the Carter Administration, evaluation of social programs suffered a decline. The middle management of the Labor Department was committed to the enactment of some version of the original Humphrey-Hawkins Act, and resources needed for the evaluation of incumbent programs were reallocated to fund demonstrations of the feasibility of the objectives of Humphrey-Hawkins—a guaranteed job for every unemployed adult. As in the 1960's, short-run considerations (getting legislation passed) dominated the long-run need for information. Available evidence that was not favorable to the goal of expanding public service employment (e.g., results that showed a high rate of fiscal substitution) was treated with enormous hostility. Unlike the 1960's, however, these new programs were never introduced, for both the Congress and the President were much too conservative to accept their basic principle—the effective abolition of the allocative function of the labor market.

Interest in the evaluation of employment and training programs did not resume when the Reagan team took over in 1981: the Reagan Administration's political philosophy holds that government intervention in the labor market, in the form of employment and training programs, is counterproductive. Thus, it was held that resources that had been allocated for such programs would be better spent by private citizens, who, with lower taxes, would save more and work harder. According to this sort of reasoning, there is no need to find out which approaches to employment and training programs work because, almost by definition, no approach works. Interestingly, the attitudes toward evaluation held by the Carter and Reagan appointees appear to have more in common than the attitudes evidenced by Nixon-Ford appointees and their two sets of successors.

Conceptual Uncertainty

A third reason why our knowledge of the impact of employment and training programs is so meager is that the underlying conceptual framework within which one must assess the impact of such programs has been in an extreme state of flux for the past decade and a half. For example, in order to assess the impact on unemployment of a program that would pay business firms a subsidy for hiring certain disadvantaged members of the work force, one must use a conceptual framework that precisely specifies why this latter group has severe unemployment problems in the first place. Any attempt to evaluate the impact of this program must specify—either explicitly or implicitly—a "model" of the operation of the labor market. If the underlying model is wrong, the evaluation results will likely be wrong.

To illustrate the reason for this, let me consider the programmatic approach that has been around the longest (and has even survived, to some extent, the Reagan team): skill retraining programs. The particular program that we will evaluate, which I will call the Training Program (TP), has the following form: Applicants who either have low earnings or are unemployed are provided classroom training for periods of six months to a year. The training provides a combination of basic and applied skills and is intended to increase participants' future employment opportunities and earnings. The traditional method of evaluating a program of this sort is to attempt to compare the post-program earnings history of participants with the earnings history of comparable non-participants. This is a difficult task, by the way, for it is impossible to verify that the comparison group is exactly (or even approximately) comparable to the experimental group. Assume, however, that it is possible to conduct a *control* group study in which participants in the program are selected randomly from the eligible population. In theory, then, it will be possible to know the true average impact of the program on participant earnings and employment. Let us assume, that the data show that the real weekly wage of participants is increased from W0 to W1 while the number of weeks they work per year are increased from E0 to E1. The total annual real earnings of the group are increased from W0 × E0 to W1 × E1. Suppose, also, that these employment and earnings increases last through the remaining worklife of each participant and that the resource cost of the program is C real dollars. Using standard benefit/cost criteria, the internal rate of return to the program is given by:

$$(1) \quad R = ((W1 \times E1) - (W0 \times E0))/C$$

In principle, internal rate of return to the program should be contrasted with the social rate of interest (a real value of 3 to 5 percent). If, for example, W1 × E1 = \$8,000 per year, while W0 × E0 = \$6,000 and C = \$20,000, then the value of R would be 10 percent, and the program would appear to be a very sound social investment.

Now, the proceeding analysis of the social costs and benefits of the TP is correct only under very special circumstances. Specifically, one must assume that (most of the time) there is continuous full employment in both the labor market into which successful participants move and the market from which they come. But suppose, instead, that the program's participants would otherwise work in a market characterized by excess unemployment at a fixed real wage (caused by, say, the federal minimum wage). Suppose, as well, that the receiving market is characterized by continuous full employment. What, in this case, will happen to total net GNP if one more participant is added to the program? There will be no loss in employment of persons associated with market 0, the source market, because, according to our assumption, the wage in the market is inflexible. However, there will be additional output equal to W1 × E1 associated with market 1. Hence, the correct internal rate of return to TP becomes

$$(2) \quad R = (W1 \times E1)/C$$

instead of equation (1). The second value for R will be much greater than the first, for the first equation incorrectly subtracts average earnings in the surplus labor source market. Using the same hypothetical values that were used previously, R will become 40 percent rather than 10 percent. These rates of return have very different policy implications.

It is interesting to point out that the conventional measure given by the first model is the *private* rate of return to training (without allowance for taxes and transfer payments). If there is an imperfection in the labor market such that W0 is institutionally (or politically) fixed, society will gain by inducing low-skilled individuals to train, although in the absence of the program the same individuals might not find similar training to be profitable. This is an "externality" of the sort that justifies government intervention in a free economy—everyone *can* be better (or at least no worse) off due to the imposition of the TP.

There are several other things that can and, in fact, do go wrong with the functioning of the labor market. One of these results from the existence of work-conditioned transfer programs, which reduce the incentives for low-skilled individuals both to remain employed in market 0 and to train for market 1. In this case, analysis of the benefits and costs associated with the TP becomes more complicated than the minimum wage example given above, but it yields an equation for the internal rate of return to the program that is a mixture (1) and (2). The important point is that a component of the return is captured by society, as a whole, and is not realized by those individuals who decided to undertake training at their own expense. Accordingly, before one can describe the results of the evaluation of TP, one must know the exact nature of the labor market environment in which the program operates.

There are several other, more general sources of conceptual uncertainty that I will mention briefly. As illustrated in Michael Wachter's chapter in this book, it is clear that the overall unemployment rate associated with labor market equilibrium (which Milton Friedman has called "the natural rate" of unemployment) has been rising over the past 30 years. Much of the justification for employment and training programs is to reduce the natural rate. I am not as confident as Wachter that we understand why the natural rate rose as much as it did or that it will not continue to rise in the next decade. One recent hypothesis is that a large fraction of the natural rate arises from sectoral shocks in the demand for different types of labor. The more frequent and the more severe these shocks are, the greater the quantity of labor required at a moment in time for labor market reallocation—hence, the higher the natural rate of unemployment.

A second hypothesis is that the economy is becoming more rigid over time, with high-paying ("good") jobs and low-paying ("bad") jobs that have similar skill requirements. The latter are often characterized by unionization and/or government employment. During the 1970's, the hourly wage gap between such jobs nearly doubled. It could be argued that this has caused high unemployment, as individuals have chosen to remain unemployed while receiving fairly high transfer payments. In Detroit, for example, some unemployed workers apparently wait for $15 per-hour jobs rather than move to Biloxi, where jobs are available at $6 per-hour.

Presently, there is also a question concerning the degree to which the overall rate of unemployment can be influenced in the short run by monetary and demand management policies. I think it is fair to assert that the prevailing Keynesian wisdom of the early 1960's—that we could "fine tune" the economy—has been proved false. However, the current popular wisdom based on the assumption of "rational expectations"—that a stable monetary policy will lead the economy fairly quickly to the natural rate—is also far from satisfactory. Thus, apart from a recognition that output and employment go up and down over the course of the business cycle, our macroeconomics tool kit is fairly empty. In my view, employment and training programs are better suited to attack long-run problems than short-run problems. Many of the new programs and shifts in program emphasis, however, have been reactions to dips in the economy. For example, bills enabling major increases in public employment were passed during the 1971 and 1975 recessions: the resulting jobs were put in place after the economy had begun its recovery. Even the recent infrastructure program, to which the Reagan Administration gave grudging support, was a response to the 1982 recession, and will not be fully in place until the middle of the present recovery.

My point is that the advice on employment and training policy that will be given to the new President in 1985 or 1989 will be no better than our understanding of the way in which labor markets work. As I have illustrated, there is much uncertainty about this subject; consequently, there must be corresponding uncertainty about the likely impact of future policies.

Some Things We Have Learned

Thus far, I have discussed what we *have not* learned about employment and training programs and why the knowledge gap persists. In the concluding section, I will emphasize three, somewhat interrelated things that we *have* learned.

Proposition 1:   At best, it is extremely difficult to operate a *national* labor market with a decentralized decision-making structure. The objectives of employment and training policy in the United States always are kept fairly mushy on purpose. The objective of increasing the employment and earnings potential of those at the low end of the income distribution, which I consider to be the only plausible justification for a labor market policy, probably is not, as a political matter, sufficient to assure the enactment of appropriate legislation. The recent history of employment and training programs suggests that the explicit and implicit goals of (i) ameliorating cyclical unemployment and (ii) providing fiscal relief for local governments had to be added to the list of objectives in order to obtain large-scale funding of the programs.

CETA is the leading example of the pitfalls associated with such confounding of objectives. If you accept my assumption that *the* problem was (and remains) the fact that a large number of adult Americans do not have sufficient skills to obtain jobs that provide what we consider to be adequate earnings, then you will want to design a program that increases the earnings and employment potential of that disadvantaged group. Local governments are only in the business of providing public services (education, safety, sanitation, etc.) at the lowest possible cost to the median voter. Ameliorating the plight of the unskilled poor—who often move between local government jurisdictions—is a *national* rather than a local government function. The decentralization of employment and training programs was an open invitation to local governments to finance normal activities that ranged from supporting community colleges to paying the salaries of firefighters with Federal Government dollars. It is not clear exactly how much "leakage" occurred in CETA, but there is no question that its magnitude was nontrivial.

The next President should be counseled *not* to support a decentralized labor market policy. If we want to shift taxation from local governments to the Federal Government, we should do so directly rather than accomplish the same end result indirectly in the name of helping the economically disadvantaged, which is a cruel hoax.

One program that attempted to circumvent this problem is the Targeted Jobs Tax Credit, which was part of the Revenue Act of 1978. The original version of this program contained only the provision of a tax credit to employers of economically disadvantaged young persons (those from families below a certain income level) and was merely an attempt to alleviate youth unemployment, especially among minorities. However, by the time the program got through Congress (which was something of a rarity for proposals from the Carter Administration), the target population had been expanded to include other groups, including AFDC recipients, convicted felons, and graduates of vocational educational programs. Program data for the first few years show that TJTC was a complete failure. I say this with a heavy heart, since I helped formulate the initial proposal. The only target group to benefit from the program in significant numbers consisted of vocational education graduates. The number of disadvantaged youth who used the program was infinitesimally small relative to the number of such individuals in the population. In short, TJTC helped only a group that did not need any help.

Why was TJTC a failure? Why did it not benefit significant numbers of disadvantaged youth? The answer probably is that the government's labeling of an individual as "disadvantaged" had a chilling effect on potential private sector employers, who concluded that a $2,000 subsidy was not sufficient to outweigh what they perceived to be the risks inherent in employing the "disadvantaged." Moreover, employers had no problem in hiring the young workers who they would have hired in any event or in getting the $2,000 in the bargain. As a result, TJTC turned out to be an inappropriate policy instrument for the alleviation of the youth employment problem.

Proposition 2: It is very difficult to target programs on those who need them most. The operational goal of offering employment and training programs to those segments of the work force that have the lowest human capital is prone to being subverted. I have already mentioned that a serious defect in the CETA jobs programs was that local government managers were motivated to use the CETA money as efficiently as they could. In the name of efficiency, they often sought to hire the best workers they could. In 1978, for example, the majority of PSE workers in one large city had completed masters degrees. Instead of "sifting through" applicants to find those who most needed work, skilled managers tended to engage in "creaming"—i.e., selecting only those applicants whose qualifications indicate that they will work productively and efficiently. One cannot blame those managers—after all, they were paid to be efficient—but the quest for efficiency, as they defined the term, ultimately subverted the goals of the CETA program.

Proposition 3: Beware of special interests. Programs that provide jobs and training for targeted groups obviously have the potential to alter the distribution of income. The decentralized American political system includes representatives of literally thousands of special, "non-needy" groups who are ready to influence legislation and administrative decisions to improve their own welfare. During the period of greatest support for labor market programs, the mid and late 1970's, any discussion of new programs or of alterations to existing ones had to take place with the demands of myriad lobbyists in mind—lobbyists whose special interests ranged from unions to various branches of local governments to business associations. There are also occupational (embodied by representatives of, for example, social workers and vocational education teachers) and regional dimensions to any decision that has to be made.

It is extremely difficult, if not impossible, to reconcile such conflicting interests with the goal of increasing the employment and earnings potential of the poorer segment of the population. Construction unions will want to make sure that nothing is built by any employment program, small business groups will push for generalized employment subsidies to firms below a certain size, representatives of county governments will argue that theirs are the most appropriate units of government to run the programs, and so on and so forth.

There has been a clear tendency for many employment and training programs to become subverted by objectives that have little or nothing to do with labor market problems. It is difficult enough to design, implement, and administer programs that attempt to help those who need help. It may be *impossible* to do so within our present political system. Programs can be established that have the *ostensible* purpose of doing good—there have been scores of these since the early 1960's—but the record to date does not suggest that they will do much good.

THREE

Alien Workers in the American Economy: Economic Consequences and Alternative Policies

Michael J. Piore
Professor of Economics
and
Mitsui Professor for Problems
of Contemporary Technology
Massachusetts Institute of Technology

Michael J. Piore received the coveted MacArthur Prize in 1984. He presently is the Mitsui Professor of Contemporary Technology at the Massachusetts Institute of Technology, where he has served since 1966. A labor economist, he received his B.A. and Ph.D. degrees from Harvard University.

Professor Piore is a member of the National Council on Employment Policy. He previously has served as consultant to the Vice President's Task Force on Youth Employment and to several agencies of the Commonwealth of Puerto Rico. He has been a member of the Panel of Factfinders of the Board of Conciliation and Arbitration of the Commonwealth of Massachusetts, the Massachusetts State Public Welfare Advisory Board, and the National Manpower Policy Task Force Associates.

He is the author of four books, including Birds of Passage: Migrant Labor and Industrial Societies, *and numerous articles.*

Introduction

Interest in immigration waxes and wanes in American politics. It has been on the rise for the past few years, spurred by a large influx of refugees, especially the Mariol Cubans, who arrived in 1980 and, for the most part, settled in Miami. Concern has been generated as well by record postwar numbers of unemployed from whom such immigrants, it is believed, are taking jobs. Immigration reform probably would have passed Congress in 1982, but for a tight legislative calendar.

The central concern in the public debate has been clandestine immigration. Estimates of the number of people in this country who lack proper documents range from 3 to 12 million. Most of these undocumented aliens are here to work, hence the concern that they take jobs from Americans. The rhetoric of the immigration debate implies, in addition, that the presence of so many illegal immigrants in direct contradiction to announced public policy represents a threat to the general social order and, hence, to the safety and security of the American public. Their ambiguous legal status certainly places the undocumented aliens, themselves, in precarious social positions, making it difficult for them to educate their children, to obtain the protection of labor legislation in the workplace, or to defend themselves against abusive landlords, money lenders, or the wrath of angry relatives, neighbors, or rejected suitors, all of whom, at any moment, can turn them over to the immigration authorities.

The Nature of Clandestine Immigration

Clandestine immigration is composed of two streams which are classified, respectively, as EWI's and visa violators. (EWI stands for *entry without inspection.*) These immigrants enter the United States surreptitiously, without any documents, mostly along the Mexican border. There also has been some entry by boat on the Florida coast, but while this has generated a considerable amount of publicity, the numbers of individuals involved must be quite small. The EWI's primarily are Mexican nationals, along with a sprinkling of migrants from other South American countries, whose numbers have been growing in response to political upheavals in those areas.

Entry without inspection is the predominant form of clandestine immigration in the West and Southwest: it is also important in the Midwest, but there it is joined by the second migration stream, visa violators. The latter immigrants enter with bonafide documents, but they violate their conditions of entry by overstaying their visas and/or by accepting gainful employment. Most members of this second group have visitor or tourist visas, but some come to the United States as students. The visitors frequently are related to United States citizens or to permanent resident aliens; a number actually come intending only to visit their relatives, but change their plans after they arrive. These visa violators make up the principle source of clandestine migration on the East Coast. They come from throughout the world, but the principle countries of origin appear to be the Dominican Republic, Colombia, and the smaller nations in the Caribbean. Undocumented Asian immigrants must also enter in this way. The conventional wisdom is that the clandestine immigrants are about evenly divided between these two streams.

A Conventional View of Immigration

The conventional view of immigration appears to be that immigrants are driven by a desperate desire to escape the poverty and depression of their home countries, which constitutes an inexorable force driving them toward the United States. Though not always made explicit, this view underlies the continual references to the economic conditions in such places as Mexico, to the population pressures in the underdeveloped worlds, and to the high rates of unemployment and/or so-called underemployment that are prevalent in such places. Given the fact that the United States is almost surrounded by poverty-stricken countries, it implies that we will be inundated with immigrants. When statistics on income levels and rates of population growth in neighboring southern countries are presented in combination with estimates of the numbers of clandestine immigrants who now are here, it seems that we have been inundated already.

Fortunately, however, there is very little evidence to support the theory that underlies such conventional wisdom. While it seems logical to conclude that the income gap between the United States and the underdeveloped world should be the basic governor of the immigration process, that does not seem to be the case.

The Sources of Immigration

The migrants are not coming from the poorest countries in the world and they are not coming from the poorest regions in their countries of origin. This remains true even when an effort is made to correct for statistics on the cost of transportation, for example, or of information about job prospects. Mexican migrants to the United States, for instance, come from places such as Jalisco, which is in the middle of the country, and from Mexico City, but not from the relatively poorer Yucatan. The poorest country in the Western Hemisphere is Haiti. It has been the poorest for many, many years; however, until quite recently, Haiti was not a principal source of migrant workers. Historically, and to a lesser extent even now, the Haitian migration has comprised primarily the relatively well-to-do and well-educated middle class.

Any theory of migration must explain its timing. The current wave of clandestine migration is recent, dating from the late 1960's. Yet, a large income differential between the United States and the countries of origin has always existed and, if anything, has probably been shrinking during this period. Similarly, it is not possible to account for recent migration flows through changes in cost differentials. Transportation costs, for example, have been remarkably stable over long periods of time. The cost of air transport from the Caribbean in the early 1970's was approximately the same percentage of an unskilled worker's weekly wage as was the cost of steamship passage from Italy in the 1880's.

Economic troubles in Mexico are thought to be augmenting undocumented migration, but this presumption also is dubious. No one seems willing to argue that undocumented migration from Mexico diminished during the Mexican oil boom of the late 1970's; if the boom did not diminish the migration, it is unclear why the present bust should augment it. However bad things may be in Mexico, one can probably do better there, surrounded by family and embedded in a community network, than in the United States, without a job and ineligible for unemployment insurance or social welfare. In any case, the argument that applies to economic refugees from Mexico also applies to political refugees from Cuba, Asia, and El Salvador: to the extent that they have a stronger motive to stay in the United States, such immigrants are likely to displace temporary migrants from other countries in the hemisphere. This displacement effect undoubtedly operates least effectively in the West, where Mexicans predominate, but strongly in the Midwest and on the East Coast, where Mexicans are only one of an immense number of different national groups who make up the immigrant population.

Immigration Control: The Conventional Views

The foregoing notion of the immigration process invites a policy of "massive resistance." To halt the "invasion," one must control both streams of clandestine immigrants, EWI's and visa violators. Control of EWI's means control of the Mexican border and leads to proposals for expanding the border patrol forces with large infusions of personnel and equipment. The incipient problem of entry along the coast would be handled by a comparable expansion of Coast Guard activities, including the interception of suspected vessels on the high seas. At times, the Coast Guard has suspended the basic civil rights and due process guarantees of suspected immigrants stopped outside United States territorial waters. Such measures also appear to be required in order to control land borders, but the constitutional issues are salient here and the scope of police activity more carefully delimited.

In principle, true border control probably is possible. The United States-Mexican border is extremely long, but mostly desert, which is difficult to cross and easy to police from the air. Most of the entry from Mexico occurs in large urban areas.

The present border patrol force is small: as Secretary Ray Marshall was fond of pointing out, smaller than the Capitol Hill police force. Current smuggling operations are relatively primitive and unorganized; more resources alone would go a long way to counter them. However, the nature of the present immigration process undoubtedly would change under the impact of a massive control operation. It is likely that there would be a corresponding adaptation of both technology and organizational effort on the other side of the border and probably a change in the locus of entry. Border control, thus, would become considerably more expensive than it appears to be at the present time. The final cost, as measured in terms of resources and, more importantly, human rights, could become quite large. However, my own opinion is that, if it were done slowly and deliberately and with a well-conceived and carefully implemented organizational structure, border control could be managed.

Visa violations, on the other hand, are a good deal more difficult to control. Almost all visa violators come to the United States for ostensibly legitimate reasons—to visit relatives, for tourism and shopping, and for education. Attempts to curtail visa violators by tightening the procedures through which visas are granted inevitably would produce untoward consequences. The consulates who issue visas are overworked and understaffed; they could easily absorb more resources. Nonetheless, it is not clear that additional resources, alone, would solve the problem. Resource constraints seem to be one of the major factors controlling the number of visas actually issued at the moment; more resources probably would make the process fairer, but might actually increase the number of visas issued. It is very difficult to judge the actual motivation of a visa applicant, and since many of those who eventually violate their visas have legitimate reasons for visiting the United States and may not even premeditate visa violation, it is not clear that clandestine immigration could be fully controlled in this way.

The difficulties of direct control—the hopelessness of controlling visa violation and the high costs of border control—have focused attention on a third proposal, "employer liability." By a quirk in the immigration legislation, employers are not responsible for checking the legal status of their employees. Reformers have argued for a long time that, if employers were charged with such responsibilities, the jobs that are attractive to clandestine immigrants would be cut off and, consequently, illegal immigration would dry up. It probably is true that this would be the case, but job control is no panacea. The exact nature of the present liability of employers has been distorted somewhat by advocates of this reform.

While it is true that employers are not liable for having undocumented workers on their payrolls, they are liable if they actively
and knowingly engage in recruitment of undocumented workers.
At times, such recruitment has been fairly widespread, albeit
circumspect. The immigration service has not been particularly
successful in developing cases against this kind of recruitment,
largely because such cases are difficult to prove without extensive
investigation, which the INS lacks the resources to conduct. More
stringent forms of liability would reduce the investigative burden,
but only marginally. For truly effective enforcement to be possible, employers would require some means of verifying the status
of job applicants. This, in turn, would require the use of national
identity cards, the contemplation of which poses apparently
insurmountable civil rights problems. Such a system would be
very expensive: budget estimates run to several millions of
dollars.

By themselves, then, employer sanctions are unlikely to have
much of an effect one way or another. To be effective, they would
require a large investment of additional resources in the INS.
Such resources could be used with nearly the same effect if they
merely were devoted to the existing bureaucratic apparatus and
used to augment investigations and INS "raids." While this much
could be done under present legislation, we have consistently
judged the cost to be too great.

Thus there is a sense in which the flood of immigrants that is
predicted by the conventional view seems to be inevitable. The
American culture seems doomed either to drown in a sea of
foreign languages and alien customs or to degenerate as the
immigrants drive down our standard of living as we divert
increasing resources to securing our borders and make progressive compromises in our basic human values in order to keep the
aliens out. Once again, however, such theories fail to withstand
the realities of the situation.

Immigrants as Temporary Workers

Insofar as I can judge from talking to immigrants, the immigration process does not work as the conventional wisdom presumes
it does, because potential immigrants view the United States

much as Americans view them. They are deeply attached to their languages and cultures and strongly rooted in their own communities, where they feel comfortable and at home. They find American society cold, alien, strange, lonely, and frightening.

Thus, their migration is not motivated by their special attraction to the United States but, paradoxically, by their commitment to their home communities. Generally, they have some particular project at home that motivates their immigration: landholdings that they would like to expand or improve; agricultural equipment or livestock that they plan to purchase; or an inter-urban taxi, shop, or a piece of industrial equipment for a home-factory in which they want to invest. Their intention is to come to the United States and work hard for a relatively short period of time, and then return home to use their accumulated earnings to finance their projects.

This, incidentally, is true not just of the current wave of foreign migration; it has been true historically as well. From what we know about the origins of the late 19th century immigrants from southern and eastern Europe, they seem to have come from areas of small landholdings, where aspirations to expand or improve their farms were widespread among peasantry. The rates at which these early migrants returned to their places of origin were quite high. Overall, 32 percent of all immigrants between 1908 and 1910 returned. For some groups, the rate was much higher: 63 percent of northern Italian migrants to the United States and 56 percent of southern Italians, for example, went home during this period.

The fact that immigrants are motivated in this way limits the range of jobs for which employers find them attractive. They are not attractive for the jobs to which adult national workers normally aspire. Such jobs require long-term commitments on the part of the labor force; high levels of education training, and experience; and a stable, regular labor force. Thus, the immigration process tends to be governed by and responds to what we call the secondary sector of the labor market: those who seek jobs that are relatively low paying and insecure, have menial social status, and lack possibilities for career advancement.

Such work is not attractive to committed national workers precisely because it has no future and adds little to the self-concept and esteem of those who perform it. Immigrants are undeterred by these same characteristics because they view their stays as temporary: they plan to leave before they are laid-off; they do not contemplate staying long enough to take advantage of career opportunities; and they obtain their self-concept from the work roles they perform at home. It is for these jobs in the secondary sector that immigrants constitute an attractive source of labor, and these jobs, in turn, control the immigration process.

Immigrants as Permanent Workers

A good many of the jobs that clandestine immigrants now hold previously were held by other immigrant groups—first by foreign immigrants from southern and eastern Europe and, subsequently, by American black workers who migrated northward from the rural South. The new foreign immigration dates from the late 1960's, when, because of the Vietnam war boom, unemployment reached extremely low levels. During that period, the labor reserves in the rural South were virtually exhausted, and the black labor force became dominated by a second generation, who had grown up in the cities.

Evidence from case studies suggests that the new generation, whose attitudes were crystallized by the civil rights movement, was perceived by employers as being intractable and difficult, if not actually dangerous, to manage. Faced with a general labor shortage and a great distrust of the existing work force, businesses began to seek new sources of labor. Increasingly, they found them among foreign workers. In a number of cases, the employers' efforts in this regard seem to have been deliberate and purposeful. Nonetheless, they went largely unnoticed, as national policy focused on obtaining higher-level jobs for blacks. In some cases, businesses actually seem to have recruited from abroad. This was the origin of the new migrant streams.

The character of an immigration stream does not remain static, however; it changes significantly over time. Most early immigrants plan to stay temporarily, but many of them end up staying longer than they intended. Some of them eventually settle permanently in the United States. Others, who finally return to their places of origin, often have children who grew up in the United States, cut off from their parents' country and deprived of cultural and linguistic ties that bind their parents to the place of origin. The long-stayers and their children form a permanent settlement, whose members, especially in the second generation, have needs and aspirations that parallel those of United States nationals.

Indeed, for practical purposes, many are United States nationals, whatever their legal status. For them, return is not a viable option. Once a permanent immigrant community forms in the United States, the circumstances facing new migrants begin to change. For example, it becomes feasible to move to the United States and settle permanently without experiencing the strangeness and cultural alienation that initially deter this kind of migration—an attraction that is not lost on potential migrants. Thus an immigration process that begins by being essentially complementary to the needs and aspirations of United States nationals generates over time a second generation as well as a growing number of first generation immigrants, who enter into direct competition with American nationals for stable jobs and careers.

The Immigrant Today

If the recent wave of immigration began in the late 1960's, it might be supposed that by this time, some 15 years later, the country has accumulated a substantial reserve of undocumented immigrants and that the originally fluid immigrant streams have begun to solidify. Much of the public discussion seems to presume that this is the case: people talk as if time alone makes the immigrant problem more and more pressing. But, whether this is true remains to be seen.

The initial upsurge of immigration in the late 1960's was a response to two factors: an unusually tight labor market, with levels of unemployment much lower than any experienced since, and a relatively sudden shift in the character of the black labor force who previously had staffed secondary jobs. The resulting shortage of workers at the bottom of the labor market created a vacuum into which the new immigrants were pulled. However, the shortage could not have increased greatly since that time, and, with rising unemployment, it actually may have shrunk.

In the last five years, there also has been a substantial infusion of refugees who have moved into jobs comparable to those previously held by undocumented migrants. But the refugees have permanent commitments to the United States which the migrants typically lack. They undoubtedly have pushed many of the migrants out of their jobs.

We know from case studies and anecdotal evidence that, however settled the original migrant communities may have become, the number who are temporary remains substantial. Because these people are here to save money, they are not interested in waiting out unemployment. They do not stay in the United States if jobs are unavailable. Indeed, as one migrant commented: "It is not worth my while to stay here if I can't hold two jobs." At their core, the immigrant communities may have become sufficiently solid to resist the pressure of unemployment and the competition from the refugees, but there still is a large number of workers at the periphery of the community who must have responded to the changing economic conditions and the new competition by going home.

Finally, what is rarely recognized in assessing the evolution of the clandestine immigrant population is that a very large proportion of those people who do settle permanently manage to legitimize their status. The official immigration system operates through a system of "equity" and "preferences" to give enormous weight to family reunification. The spouses, parents, and children under the age of 21 of United States citizens are admitted outside of the official quotas. Moreover, the preference system allocates 20 percent of the overall quota of 270,000 immigrants to unmarried sons and daughters of United States citizens, 26 percent to unmarried sons and daughters of permanent resident aliens, 10 percent to married sons and daughters of citizens and 24 percent to brothers and sisters of citizens.

Very few people develop a desire to settle permanently in an area without also developing the social and family ties that eventually qualify them for permanent immigration visas under one or another of these various family unification provisions. Indeed, most visa violators come to the United States as family visitors who already possess these kinds of ties. It is common practice for undocumented aliens to apply for official admission, come to the United States, live and work clandestinely while their applications are pending, and then return home when their applications are granted in order to enter the United States legally. In this way, documented and undocumented migration are intertwined, and the pool of undocumented workers is continually diminished by official immigration.

The estimate of the stock of undocumented migrants has remained unchanged at 3 to 12 million since the early 1970's. It is generally supposed that this is due to the width of the range estimated, and that the true figure has moved upward over time. Given rising unemployment, the competition of refugees, and the processes of legitimation through official immigration, however, the true figure might just as well have declined.

Immigration Policy

What does this alternative view of immigration imply for public policy? The major concern of policymakers has been the threat that immigration poses to the income and employment opportunities of American nationals. In the conventional understanding, the immigrants constitute a generalized threat. In the process just sketched out, the threat is much more limited and confined. The immigrants, at least in the early stages of the process, do not threaten the employment opportunities of permanent adult workers, particularly those in jobs requiring long-term career commitments. Indeed, insofar as a certain amount of menial, unskilled, and insecure work is necessary to sustain stable, long-term job opportunities, the immigrants actually may complement national workers who hold more desirable jobs.

The competition occurs between the immigrants and other marginally committed labor force groups, particularly youth and secondary women workers, whose primary commitments are to home and family responsibilities. Even that kind of competition is difficult to assess. The nature of the labor force commitments of these groups is, itself, ambiguous. Moreover, the jobs at stake are in competition with foreign producers, and any attempt to replace the immigrant labor force with nationals might simply drive such jobs abroad.

The difficulties for analysis and policy formulation are illustrated by two studies, just nearing completion, of New York City industries: one, by Tom Bailey, of immigrants in the New York City restaurant industry; the second, by Roger Waldinger, of the New York City garment industry. In the restaurant industry, immigrants tend to be concentrated in a distinct sector comprising ethnic restaurants that are owned and managed by immigrant entrepreneurs. This sector coexists with two other sectors: the fast-food sector—typified by McDonald's, which is staffed primarily with young, part-time workers—and full-service restaurants, owned by American nationals who employ some immigrants but also a number of nationals who are typified in New York by aspiring actors and actresses.

On the basis of a comparison with other cities that have much smaller immigrant groups, Bailey argues that the competition between immigrants and nationals is not a direct one but one that occurs through the relative sizes of these different sectors. Without the immigrants, he argues, the fast-food sector would be much larger: McDonald's would substitute for the Greek coffee shop at the bottom of the price line and limited-menu steak houses would substitute at the top. This is partly a substitution of youth for immigrant labor. Nonetheless, a good deal of the fast-food operation is industrial: food and equipment are prepared in remote manufacturing establishments, which tend to offer relatively unskilled jobs that are accessible to immigrants—jobs with hours and locations that are not attractive to youth. Moreover, such manufacturing activities can be performed easily abroad.

Clearly, the jobs lost by immigrants would not be converted to youth restaurant jobs on a one-for-one basis. It is not completely clear that youth could be attracted to fill even new restaurant jobs that would be created by curtailing immigration. The restaurants in the non-immigrant cities that Bailey examined have dispersed populations and family clienteles. They are located near the youth whom they employ. New York City restaurants have professional and business clienteles and are located in the center city, remote from the residence of young workers.

Employment patterns in the garment industry are equally complicated and ambiguous. Waldinger argues that the New York garment industry caters to a particular segment of the national market. It concentrates on the production of short runs of specialty items for spot markets. Therefore, it needs the large, flexible source of labor that immigrants provide. The immigrant communities also provide a certain continuity of skill, which otherwise is difficult to maintain and which is particularly important, given the type of production in which the city specializes.

Outside of the city, production is of a very different sort: it consists of much longer runs of products that are more standard (the contrast here is between blue jeans and dresses) and/or ordered in advance (a successful style might, for example, be produced and stocked outside of New York City at the beginning of the season and then reordered in small, rush batches from city factories to meet unexpected demand later on). Longer production runs originally were done in New York, but because such work requires less skill, benefits from large production facilities, and is compatible with the time delays involved in shipping from remote locations, most of it moved out of the city during the postwar decades, first to rural areas in the United States and then abroad. With the new immigration, a little of it has begun to come back to the city.

It is difficult to imagine the industry without a fashion center such as New York and the "spot market" segment of the industry that resides there. New York's chief American competitors are Miami and Los Angeles, both of which use similar immigrant labor forces; without any immigrants, the whole industry might move abroad. The recent return of long production runs to the city has occurred, in part, at the expense of farm wives in rural Pennsylvania, upstate New York, and the South. In this sense, the immigrants occasionally do compete with American nationals. But it has also occurred at the expense of foreign producers; the domestic production that moved to New York might otherwise have moved abroad. The significance of the jobs lost to the farm wives is also debatable. Before the factories moved into those areas, most of the present employees had never considered working: The rural labor force was a creation of employers in much the same way that the immigrant labor force in the city is a product of employer recruiting.

Taken together, these considerations lead me to conclude that the concern that has motivated current legislative proposals is misplaced and that the legislation, itself, is ill-conceived. I would argue that we ought, nonetheless, to make an effort to limit and control the immigration process. The reason for doing so is that, over a very long period of time, uncontrolled immigration does have the capacity to erode the employment opportunities of national workers and that, generally, a tight market in which labor is in short supply is more conducive to social progress than is a loose one.

The best way to limit immigration, however, is by direct control over employment conditions, by raising wages and improving working conditions on the jobs to which immigrants are attracted in the hope that nationals eventually will be attracted in their place. Policy instruments for doing this are available in our labor standards legislation and in the National Labor Relations Act. Therefore, I would devote the resources that we currently are talking about devoting to the enforcement of immigration legislation to the enforcement of labor legislation and to legislative reforms that would raise the minimum wage, facilitate union organization, tighten health and safety standards, and the like.

I prefer this to tighter immigration legislation because, in general, I think it is more humane—more consistent with the preservation of and respect for human rights—to control jobs rather than people. I also think that the immigration debate tends to become entangled in feelings of xenophobia and racism, which obscure the underlying economic interests at stake. As a result, we are systematically led to pass legislation that we are unwilling to enforce when we see its economic costs. A debate that focuses upon the minimum wage and labor standards legislation makes such costs much more salient.

I take it as axiomatic that if we are unwilling to support legislation that directly raises the cost of labor, we should be unwilling to enforce immigration legislation that has the effect of doing this indirectly by removing the foreign labor force. On the other hand, it is a consistent part of this policy not only to enforce labor standards directly but also to combine that form of enforcement with enforcement of immigration legislation through periodic raids on establishments known to employ clandestine immigrants in order to regularly vacate their jobs, open them up to nationals, and test their "desirability."

It would be a great mistake to see a solution to any of our basic economic and social problems in the control of immigration. This seems obvious to me, given the high levels of unemployment we currently are experiencing, although, given the rhetoric surround-

ing it, the point is worth emphasizing. Current unemployment is
the product of a deep, prolonged economic recession and long-
term structural adjustments in the technologies and international
competitive positions of our major industries. The increases in
unemployment have been concentrated precisely among the committed adult male workers who are *not* in competition with
immigrants. The low-wage, unstable, menial jobs that the immigrants hold will not substitute for the jobs the unemployed have
lost.

It is true that immigrants' jobs might ease their adjustment
problems if the displaced workers were willing to take them, but
few of the displaced workers are willing to accept the humiliation
of such a major decline in social status for the relatively small
amount of income involved. A real solution to the present unemployment problems will require both an economic recovery and
training and relocation assistance to help permanently displaced
workers find dignified places within the economy.

A similar point can be made with respect to black youth. A
number of the jobs now held by immigrants once were held by
black nationals. If the immigrants were somehow to disappear,
black nationals would again take over some of their former jobs.
However, the immigrants did not *displace* blacks. Employers
perceived a change in blacks' attitudes toward work—a change
that made them difficult and dangerous to manage—and they
recruited immigrants to replace them. Black attitudes changed
because an older generation, raised in the rural South with a
background and motivation similar to the immigrants', was
replaced by a new generation who grew up in the urban North.
These younger workers associated their parents' jobs with the
inferior status to which their race had been condemned in America and feared that they would be confined in them permanently
through prejudice and discrimination; thus, they sought higher-
status jobs.

This process of replacement occurred almost 15 years ago in a
much tighter labor market—at a time when both the political
climate and the levels of welfare and other social benefits were
much more conducive to such attitudes than they are today. It is
likely that black workers' resistance to such work has moderated
somewhat. This is the case for pressing to reopen some of these
jobs. But neither I nor, more importantly, the business executives

involved believe that the attitudes have changed substantially. The real solution to the employment problems of blacks requires upward social mobility.

Finally, precisely because of the experience with the black revolt in the 1960's, it would be a great mistake to attempt to control immigration by directly forestalling settlement. The black movement was essentially a revolt of second-generation immigrants—a revolt of the children of a generation who had come up out of the South, who were no longer satisfied with their parents' jobs, but who did not have access to the high wages and career opportunities that might have satisfied their aspirations.

Prejudice and discrimination were undoubtedly major factors blocking their advancement, but the black youth of the 1960's were also poorly trained for the positions to which they aspired. The children of the new immigrants undoubtedly will view their parents' jobs in much the same way that the blacks did, and they may react in much the same way if their own advancement is thwarted. Any attempt to prevent their parents from settling permanently will bar the children from access to the educational and cultural facilities that will enable them to fulfill their aspirations and will recreate for another major portion of our population the social tensions that have permeated black communities for the last 20 years.

American society has a moral obligation to these children. They are here because we wanted the labor of the parents; in a very real sense, we recruited their parents. By doing so, we cast the children in the American mold: they probably are more like us in terms of their values and aspirations and even their culture and language than they are like their parents. Having cast them in our mold, we have an obligation to treat them as we would treat our own children. In the process, we may create competitors for our children. This may be an argument for more careful control of the use of immigrant labor in the secondary sector, but it is not a very strong argument for limiting the aftereffects of that immigration by pressing on the children, who, like us, have nowhere else to go.

To limit policy in this way does not imply that we must accept the settlement process as being inevitable and beyond our control. That process can be limited in a variety of ways. Higher wages, which act to attract American nationals to jobs, will also limit settlement by enabling temporary immigrants to meet their target earnings more rapidly and return home before they develop permanent attachments to the United States.

Economic development in the home countries will also limit settlement in the United States. Certain visa policies can have important effects on settlement: time limitations on visitors' visas, paradoxically, encourage long stays because visa violators are reluctant to return home after their visas have expired for fear that they will not be permitted to return to the United States. We could prevent new migration streams from starting by placing greater reliance on investigation and strategic enforcement in border control activities, the surveillance of immigrant communities in the United States, and in granting visitors' visas abroad.

These policies are all a good deal more humane than those contemplated in the current legislative debate; and they are less costly, as well. I think that such policies ultimately will be more effective in preserving the economic and spiritual values of Americans.

FOUR

Science, Technology, and Employment: The Reindustrialization of America

Joe B. Wyatt
Chancellor
Vanderbilt University

Joe B. Wyatt is Chancellor of Vanderbilt University. In addition, he serves in such capacities as: Chairman of the Advisory Committee for Information Science and Technology, National Science Foundation; Editor in Chief of the Journal for Applied Management Systems; *Vice Chairman of the Board of Directors and Chairman of the Investment Committee of the Massachusetts Technology Development Corporation; Member of the Policy Board of the National Association of Independent Colleges; Fellow of Gallaudet College; and Chairman of the Advisory Committee on Technology in Education of the Office of Technology Assessment.*

Chancellor Wyatt is a member of Sigma Xi, Beta Gamma Sigma, The American Association for the Advancement of Science, The Institute of Electrical and Electronic Engineers, and The Association for Computing Machinery. He has degrees in mathematics from the University of Texas and Texas Christian University, and has contributed frequently to the literature on modern technology. Most notable have been his works on the use of computer systems in university administration.

Introduction

In the *Wall Street Journal* of February 3, 1983 there appeared a feature article summarizing various economists' projections for economic recovery during 1983. Forty-five forecasters, virtually everyone who is anyone in the business of economic forecasting, were quoted—from the President's Economic Advisor, Martin Feldstein, to such corporate forecasters as Chase, Wharton, and DRI. The forecasters' predictions differed widely: the rate of growth in GNP forecasted for 1983 ranged from 1.4 percent to 4.9 percent, after adjustment for inflation. Mr. Feldstein brought in the most cautious forecast of 1.4 percent. One of the most optimistic of the forty-five was Richard Karfunkle (Econoviews International, Inc.) who captured my attention more with an observation about economic forecasting than with his prediction of 4.5 percent growth. Mr. Karfunkle says that he makes his economic projections on the back of an envelope, because "you can erase a lot faster on the back of an envelope." As if to support the Karfunkle hypothesis, Feldstein raised his forecast dramatically within the week.

This essay began on the backs of envelopes, with notes scribbled at various times to be fleshed out or discarded later—a habit of mine developed years ago. But Mr. Karfunkle may have identified the major benefit of writing on the backs of envelopes, at least for a topic as full of uncertainty as that of this essay.

My objective is to place in some perspective the future effects of science and technology on employment. However, I am more likely to provide clues that will lead readers to their own eventual conclusions than I am to set forth crisp and lasting answers to questions that are just beginning to take shape.

Perspective On Technology

Technology, the implementation of scientific discovery, is contributing substantially to an employment crisis in the United States; a crisis that seems likely to increase in complexity and intensity well into the 21st century. The phenomena resulting from this crisis will range over the broadest spectrum of employment issues: from the displacement of skilled and semi-skilled workers by robots to serious shortages of scientists, engineers, educators, and authors, whose skills will be needed to develop new knowledge and to communicate that knowledge effectively to the rest of the population. Virtually all parts of the United States economy are affected by this crisis, although some parts appear to be more seriously troubled than others.

From an historical perspective, the 100-year movement from the farm to the factory—from an agrarian economy to an industrial revolution, economic, social, and political—continues to be assessed, even romanticized, in search of clues that will guide us in our current transition. The move from an agrarian to an industrial economy in America resulted from the emergence of a technology that magnified human muscle power, beginning generally with the steam engine perfected by James Watt some 200 years ago. Further refinements of "mechanical engine power," notably the internal combustion engine powered by liquid fossil fuels, decentralized the application of basic industries, particularly agriculture. As a result, the mechanized agrarian began to achieve productivity gains that allowed overall farm output to increase, even as vast numbers of farm workers moved from the farms to the factories of industrialized America. Indeed, the contemporary American farmer embodies one of the world's great achievements in productivity achieved through technology.

The technology that transformed farming methods—the tractors, seed drills, cultivators, and harvesting equipment; the trucks and trains that allowed the movement of farm products over greater distances; the commercial fertilizers and insecticides; and other developments—filled out the major elements of a highly automated American food production system. All of these elements, essential to the growth in productivity of the farmer, were the progeny of factories that were developed in the large industrial centers of America and powered by mechanical and electrical engines that augmented human muscle power. They achieved economies of scale in the mass production of "raw materials," including steel and rubber, that benefited other factories that produced finished machines to be used to further refine and develop the industrial and agrarian systems of America. Viewed in the larger perspective, the contribution of each individual worker, whether on the farm or in the factory, continued to improve steadily and surely. The great wars, beginning with the Civil War, stimulated industrialization by demanding the production of weapons—weapons that increased in sophistication and quantity as the means to produce them, the industrialized factories, also improved in sophistication and productivity.

Now, the "industrial age" in America is giving way to an economy based on services and information. Many feel that the resulting employment effects will be as significant as those experienced in the United States' move from an agricultural economy to an industrial economy. Regardless of the effects, today's changes are occurring at a much faster rate than did the change to the industrial economy (Figure 1).

I propose to characterize the move from an agrarian economy to an industrial economy and, thence, to a service economy as a logical continuance of the interplay among technology, mind, and muscle. While it is not my purpose to pose semantic arguments about the widespread use of the terms "industrial revolution" and, now, "technological revolution," I believe that such terms suggest a spontaneity and an unpredictability that limit, rather

Figure 1
Percent of United States Labor Force in Service,
Goods-Producing, and Agricultural Industries.

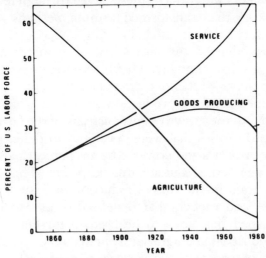

than promote, an understanding of the underlying phenoma. For example, the industrial revolution did not spell the end of agriculture. Far from it.

The production of food has continued to increase, both in the United States and worldwide, as the population has increased. The increase has been virtually monotonic over more than two centuries. What happened over those two centuries was the result of improved agricultural productivity that resulted, in turn, from the application and refinement of various technologies. The resulting productivity gains allow orders of magnitude more food to be produced by orders of magnitude fewer people. Future technological refinements in agriculture, perhaps most notably in the field of plant genetics, continue to promise further improvements.

The same basic interplay among mind, muscle, and technology produced similar productivity gains in the industrial economy: orders of magnitude more production has been obtained from the efforts of orders of magnitude fewer workers. In other words, the coming death of the industrial economy does not signal less industry or fewer products; it is a signal of improvement in the productivity of each worker through the ingenious application of, primarily, technology. The most important technological development, the one that has affected, and continues to affect, virtually all recent technological developments is the computer. Coupled with basic science, mathematics, and engineering, the computer has produced a watershed of technology that fills human wants and needs in ways that alter the composition and makeup of the American work force at all levels.

Let me summarize and project the development of the computer, for it is the newest member of the employable population—a member that promises to magnify the powers of the human mind and even to displace its use in some respects. In the 1940's, John Von Neumann, working in a context established by several predecessors decades earlier, notably Turing and Babbage, conceived and specified the stored-program digital computer, the concept upon which the design of all contemporary digital computers is based. Early applications of the Von Neumann concepts using telephone relays and vacuum tubes for hardware, together with programs that were primitive by today's standards, demonstrated the feasibility of the concept in several university and industrial laboratories. By the early 1950's, the first commercial digital computers were introduced to the marketplace by IBM (the 701) and Sperry Rand (the Univac I). To hark back to the fallibility of economic projections and Mr. Karfunkle's back-of-the-envelope hypothesis, market projections made at the time the IBM 701 and the Univac I were introduced predicted a worldwide demand for fewer than 50 computers!

The Forester group's invention of magnetic core memory at MIT in the early 1950's, the Shockley group's invention of the transistor at about the same time, the Noyce group's conception of the integrated circuit chip in 1950, the doubling each year of chip complexity, which has enabled the microcomputer-on-a-chip—all have accelerated the development of the computer and its application beyond any previous projection. Today's micro-computer is tiny, portable, and reliable. It can be packaged to withstand virtually any environmental condition. Its storage capacity and its speed continue to rise rapidly, and its cost continues to decline.

Figure 2 provides some perspective on the magnitude of past, present, and future improvements.

According to sociologist Daniel Bell, citizens of the 21st cen-

Figure 2
The Magnitude of Past, Present, and Future Improvements in Microcomputers.

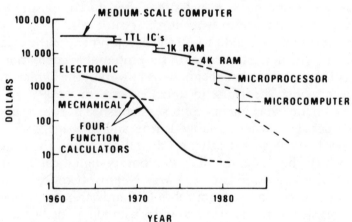

tury probably will view miniaturization as the most extraordinary technological development of our time.

The amount of time presently needed to develop enabling software, the contemporary term for sets of programs for computers, poses occasional delays in the application of computers to specific problems, but such delays are only temporary. And as software is perfected to perform a particular function, using a particular computer, copies can be "manufactured" and distributed at low cost.

Some Applications of Technology

The computer has played dual roles in the development of new science and new technology: first, as a research instrument that allows the modelling and testing of scientific phenomena through mathematics and engineering; and, second, as a primary component of specific devices. The advent of the microcomputer has accelerated both roles. As the computer has developed continuously through research and experimentation over the past four decades, it has joined other threads of research from other disciplines to produce a watershed of technology. Consider one recent example.

About the time the Von Neumann concepts were being formulated in 1946, Edward Purcell and Felix Bloch, working independently, discovered a phenomenon called Nuclear Magnetic Resonance, a technique for probing the properties of atomic nuclei. The technique permits observation of the fact that hydrogen, phosphorous, and other elements having an odd number of protons or neutrons produce different electromagnetic responses to the momentary application of a strong magnetic field. Independent developments including the design of magnets with stronger and more uniform magnetic fields, work in mathematics by John Tukey that led to a breakthrough in computer algorithms for Fourier transforms, Lauterbur's experiments that suggested localization of NMR signals by using field gradients—each a separate thread of scientific discovery—have led to the technology of Nuclear Magnetic Resonance Imaging. NMR imaging devices, themselves, could not function without their high-speed, high-capacity microcomputer components.

Some of the potential effects of NMR imaging technology include the following:

1. It promises to render obsolete a prior "breakthrough" in medical diagnostic technology, the X-ray CAT Scanner, that has been deployed for less than a decade and in which billions of dollars have been invested worldwide.
2. The production and widespread application of NMR imaging may displace a variety of skilled workers ranging from physicians to technicians. It will, at least, necessitate the re-education of radiologists and will cause an alteration of medical school curricula. It may also alter the mix of medical services, including surgery.
3. The design, development, and production of NMR imaging devices and related equipment will create a multi-billion dollar industry and a consequent demand for new job skills (e.g., in the production of large, "pure" magnets) as well as new demands for existing job skills (e.g., microcomputer production). The NMR industry will produce another contest between American and foreign manufacturers for market superiority. NMR is but one example of hundreds of new technological developments that form the basis for America's hopes for a new wave of economic development that, in turn, may affect the employment of its people at all levels.

Consider another example. A set of seemingly unrelated discoveries over the past 30 years in biological research recently have been combined to produce, perhaps, the newest form of "technological revolution", biotechnology. Among its early effects was the release for sale in September, 1982 of human insulin manufactured by a process that uses recombinant DNA technology. Dozens of products from biotechnology are now undergoing clinical or animal tests. Included among these are interferon, human growth hormone, and a vaccine for foot-and-mouth disease.

The application of recombinant DNA techniques to plant tissue is underway. Microorganisms can now be used to produce antibiotics as well as special chemical components such as amino acids. The field is so new that, aside from the dazzling successes of a few new business ventures such as Genentech and Biogen, the future employment effects are unclear. It is clear, however, that a variety of skills in science and technology will be required of most participants in this emerging market for workers in research, development, and manufacture. It seems clear that the biotechnology industry will contribute significantly to the creation of new jobs. However, it is also interesting to note that many of the prototypical manufacturing processes used in biotechnology have been highly automated through the use of computer technology. More automation in production is virtually certain after these prototypes have been proven.

Technology and Employment: The Present

In the industrial economy of past decades, particularly in the years prior to 1965, America was dominant in all phases of business: research and development, manufacturing, marketing, and product application.

During this period, a substantial part of the American work force was involved in the manufacturing sector. In the decade 1955 to 1965, prototype technology was developed that signaled the end of an era in mass production as well as the end of many of the jobs that were associated with large-scale assembly line methods of manufacturing. The two major ingredients of this prototype technology were the computer and the machine tool. Developed at MIT by a special project team staffed by personnel from aerospace companies and MIT, the prototype system was demonstrated in 1958. It allowed mechanical engineering designs to be represented in a new computer programming language called APT. The APT language contained commands for the mathematical definition of part geometry as well as commands for directing the path of a cutting tool within the context of the defined geometry.

Over several years' time, computer programs were developed that were able to interpret the APT language definitions and instructions to produce ordered sequences of incremental motion commands for a machine tool. The use of these "computer-controlled machine tools" spread rapidly throughout the American aerospace industry, with the capital cost largely financed by the United States Government. Once a link was forged between the representation, in computer language, of geometric forms derived from engineering designs and the machines that could manufacture the parts, the race to build automatic factories had begun.

In the 25 years that followed, the computer-controlled machine tool technology was joined and augmented by a second technology, called computer-aided design and manufacture (CAD/CAM). The resulting combination of technologies, enabled by further developments in computer hardware and software, has become known as Flexible Manufacturing Systems (FMS), which is the essence of the automated factory. In March of 1983, almost exactly 25 years after the prototype demonstration of APT at MIT, a new Japanese factory, owned by the Yamazaki Company and employing FMS, will start production. A brief description of the Yamazaki factory, from *Fortune* magazine of February 21, 1983, is as follows:

> *"The new plant's 65 computer-controlled machine tools and 34 robots will be linked via a fiber-optic cable with the computerized design center back in headquarters. From there the flexible factory can be directed to manufacture the required types of parts—as well as to make the tools and fixtures to produce the parts—by entering into the computer's memory the names of various machine tool models scheduled to be produced and pressing a few buttons to get production going. The Yamazaki plant will be the world's first automated factory to be run by telephone from corporate headquarters.*
>
> *The plant will have workmen, to be sure: 215 men helping produce what would take 2,500 in a conventional factory. At maximum capacity the plant will be able to turn out about $230 million of machine tools a year. But production is so organized that sales can be reduced to $80 million a year, if need be, without laying off workers."*

The *Fortune* article goes on to state that such factories typically can produce in three days the number of parts that would require three months to produce using conventional machines operated by skilled workers. Yamazaki estimates that, over five years of operation, the plant will produce after-tax profits of $12 million, compared with $800,000 for a conventional plant. This methodology also enables small-volume production runs without retooling—reprogramming the computer-controlled machines does the trick. And, of course, the products of this FMS factory are parts that are used to produce other machines, including other robots. Compared with manufacturing technology of only a decade ago, the automated plant is 15 times more profitable and 30 times more productive, and requires 10 times fewer people to operate.

History is repeating itself. Just as the work force once was displaced from the farm to the factory, manufacturing workers are on the verge of being displaced from the factory. And just as technology has continued to improve farm productivity, it promises to improve factory productivity, perhaps even more.

This time, however, most of the productivity gains can be attributed to the computer, the technology that magnifies the power of the human mind. Its refinements, when coupled with biotechnology and the ever more sophisticated machinery that magnifies human muscle power, will lead to productivity improvements that are difficult to contemplate and virtually impossible to forecast with accuracy.

Technology and Employment: The Future

There can be no doubt that the development and implementation of new technology will have substantial effects on employment in America. Indeed, these effects will be felt worldwide—a fact that cannot be overlooked in considering the future of employment in America. For example, it is clear that Japan and Western Europe intend to capture a greater share of the market in the technology-based industries, and are doing so already. Japan, particularly, has been able to reallocate capital and labor, while quickly adopting productivity-enhancing technologies. The Japanese economy is characterized by rapid growth. Such reallocations and displacements are much easier to accomodate in a growing economy; the United States passed up most of its opportunities for similar advances in the 1960's and 1970's, particularly in the steel and auto industries. Without strong economic growth to create new jobs for displaced workers and to absorb new, relatively unskilled workers, the effects of rapid technological change on employment are much more difficult to digest.

It is difficult to forecast economic growth, particularly in the short run. The best of our economic forecasters, using thousands of data elements and a variety of sophisticated tools, are unable to agree on GNP growth rates for 1983. In the long run, however, there does seem to be some general agreement that the world markets have enormous capacities to absorb new technologies that have been and continue to be, invented in America. It is clear from recent experience, however, that America's talent for developing new technologies does not lead invariably to the lion's share of the world market for the products and services that can be produced using those technologies. Several other countries, including, primarily, Japan have demonstrated their superiority in enlarging their industrial market shares by exploiting American technological developments. The most crucial issue affecting long-run future employment in America probably is the manner in which America responds to the phenomenon that some have called "the Japanese Sputnik."

New England may provide a useful model for contemplating such a response. Having been involved there for the past 10 years, I have concluded that some elements of America's future success may be discovered by contemplating a nation-wide application of the principles that have "rejuvenated" the New England economy. In 1972, the New England economy was described as "decaying." By 1975, New England's unemployment rate was over 10 percent; nationwide, unemployment stood at 8.4 percent. Although it remained elevated for most of the decade, by September of 1982, Boston's unemployment rate had declined to 6.4 percent—lower than the national average and lower than Houston's 8.2 percent and Los Angeles' 9.4 percent. Forty percent of the new jobs that were created during Massachusetts' economic recovery were in electronics, computers, drugs, aerospace, instrumentation, and weaponry—the so-called "high technology" industries. Most of the remaining positions were in the "service" industries.

Growth rates for manufacturing employment in New England's high technology industries between 1975 and 1980 included: Vermont (48.2 percent); Massachusetts (40.2 percent); Rhode Island (26.2 percent); and Connecticut (23.2 percent).

Over the same five-year period, the growth rate for California was 42.9 percent; for Florida it was 56.9 percent. For Illinois and

Ohio, though, the growth rates were only 3.1 percent and 1.7 percent, respectively. If one has faith in projections, Ohio may take heart. *The Omni Future Almanac of 1983* predicts that Columbus, Ohio will be among six cities in the world to "challenge Japan and Silicon Valley for the leading role in Applied Science discovery and achievement."

At present, however, New England appears to be succeeding at a process, begun three centuries ago, of shifting the essence of its economy from agrarian to industrial to technological. In the early part of this century, New England experienced the demise of industries that were based on the scale economics of the industrial revolution—principally textiles, shoes, and apparel. Many of the new electronics and computer companies occupy spaces in the sturdily constructed old textile mills that have lain empty for years, but now provide cheap space for fledgling companies.

What are the prerequisites for the successful economic changes that New England and a few other states are leading?

1. *The availability of venture capital and a good business climate for new, high-risk ventures.* The economic recovery of the high tech industries in Massachusetts did not begin in the 1970's until venture capital for startups and relatively high-risk second stage financings became available. In 1982, *Venture Capital Journal* estimated that over 60 percent of new investment venture capital in America went to California, Massachusetts, New York, and Texas. Risks certainly exist—the number of bankruptcies and the number of startups in Massachusetts run neck and neck.

2. *The existence of strong educational systems.* The public and private educational systems in New England are very strong at all levels, but particularly strong in higher education. The public primary and secondary schools in Massachusetts are among the best in the world, and so are the private schools. Continuing education programs for adults are robust and well subscribed, ranging from the extensive programs at Harvard University to the very sizable programs offered by the regional technical high schools in Massachusetts.

3. *The availability of a well-educated, adaptable, competitively priced work force at all levels of employment.* In 1980, Massachusetts' average manufacturing wage was just over half that of Michigan, even though both states have extensive organized labor forces. Large numbers of high-tech workers, from technicians to Ph.D.'s, migrate around New England, moving from

company to company, building their skills and taking them as
they go with the ebb and flow of business success and failure.
Illiteracy is very low, and most workers have multiple skills that
allow them to work at "fill-in" jobs during times of unemployment—a situation that existed often from 1965 to 1975.

4. *Close cooperation among government, business, and education.*
New England's marks are spotty on this essential criterion. High
taxes and poor government services, at one point, pushed relationships to the breaking point in Massachusetts, Connecticut,
and Rhode Island. Both individuals and companies fled to nearby
New Hampshire and Vermont to avoid those problems. A con-
certed and generally successful effort to improve communication
and cooperation among state government, business, and education in Massachusetts began in the mid-1970's and continues
today. It was critical to the recent economic recovery.

Several other characteristics that are desirable for the development of "technology-based" industries are not uniformly
present in New England. For example, energy costs and energy
consumption are high because of New England's northern lati-
tude. It seems clear that such negative factors are being out-
weighed by the positive one; however, history has shown this to
be a delicate balance, worthy of constant attention. Nonetheless,
it is abundantly clear that mature and productive relationships
among business, government, and education are fundamental
requirements for success.

With manufacturing employment in decline and with the
future demand for labor occurring in services, service-related,
and "high-tech" industries, what is the future for employment in
America? Perhaps the new members of the work force can
inform us. Consider the population of 18-year-olds in the United
States for each year from 1960 to 2000 (see Fig. 3). Except for
mortality and immigration, the 18-year-old population is deterministic for the period in question. The increase in the size of
this age cohort that began in 1950 peaked in 1979. Thus, the
population of 18-year-olds will decline by about 30 percent over
the next dozen years, bottoming out in the mid-1990's. A new
surge in the birth rate has produced children who will reach age
18 by the turn of the 21st century. Those children presently are
enrolled in our primary schools. But, for a critical period of our
future, the supply of young workers, including new college

Figure 3
Annual Projections of 18-Year-Olds in the United States.

graduates, will decline significantly. On average, the American work force will grow older (see Fig. 4).

It is instructive to note the major fields of study that were chosen by college graduates who entered the work force over the past seven years, as the nation entered the "technological age." Of the total number of degrees awarded by American universities over the past seven years (see Fig. 5), the largest major field, in absolute numbers, is education. The past several years have

Figure 4
America is Getting Older.

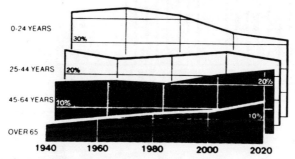

More people are approaching the age when they will receive Social Security benefits with fewer people to pay into the system.

Figure 5 Total Degrees Awarded (all fields).

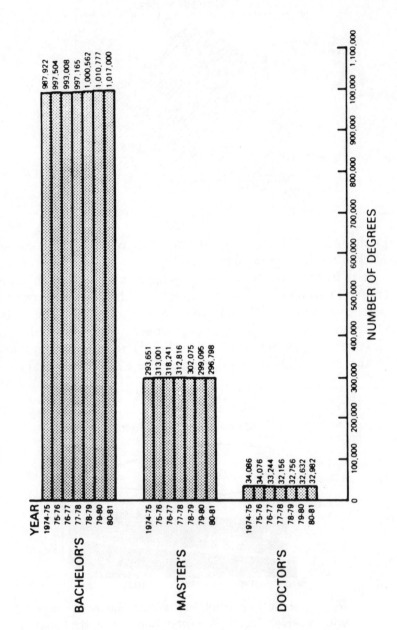

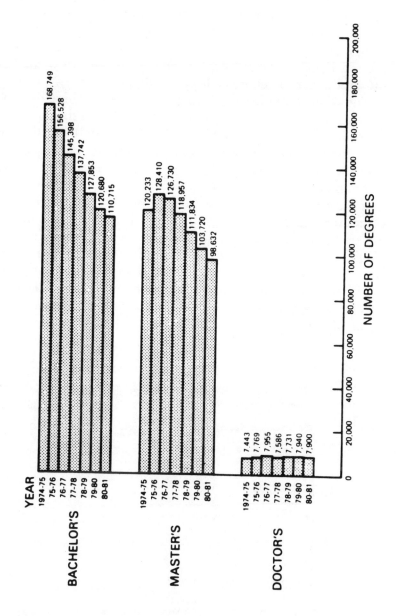

Figure 6 Degrees Awarded in Education.

seen a rapid decline in that number (see Fig. 6). The next largest category is business and management, a major field that shows a rapid increase over the same period (see Fig. 7). The next five largest fields, all of which are declining rapidly, are the social sciences, letters, psychology and history (Fig. 8). The most rapidly growing fields, in terms of student majors, are led by computer science (a tripling over seven years), mechanical and chemical engineering (a doubling), and the electrical engineering group (an increase of 50 percent). (See Fig. 9).

The rapid growth is occurring in the fields where one could expect it to occur in a "technological age." But, in absolute terms, the total number of computer science majors in the peak year of 1981 was less than the number of history majors, about one-third the number of psychology majors, and only about 15 percent of the number of education majors.

It is estimated that, for the foreseeable future, the demand for computer-science-trained graduates will exceed the supply by 50,000 annually. Indeed, two years ago it was estimated that a single American company had needs for computer science majors in excess of the nation's total supply for that year of graduating students with baccalaureate and masters degrees in that field. Other data show that, for virtually all post-secondary fields of study, computer-literate job applicants have a decided

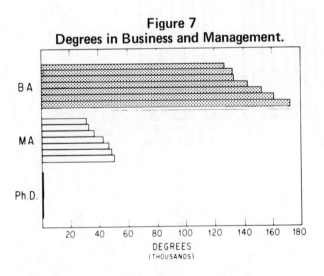

Figure 7
Degrees in Business and Management.

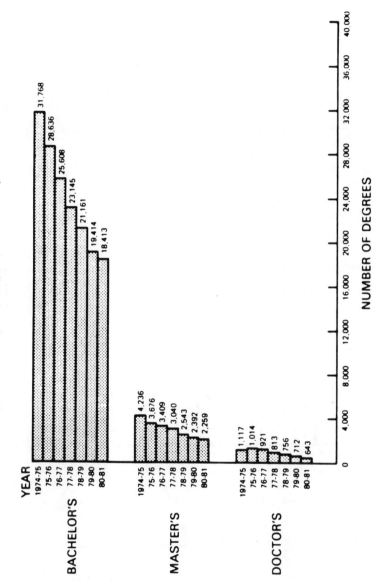

Figure 8   Degrees Awarded in History.

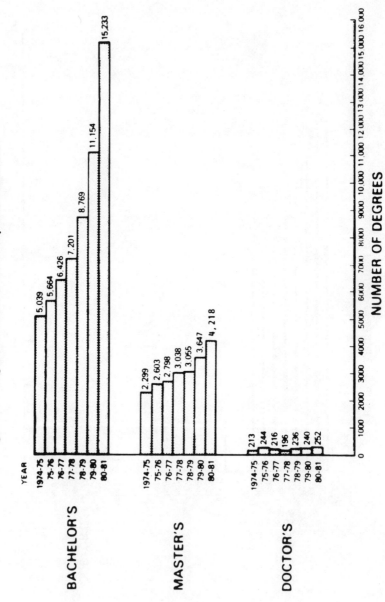

Figure 9   Degrees Awarded in Computer Science.

advantage over others in the competition for jobs. This is also the case for job applicants who lack college degrees or high school diplomas—who constitute a much larger number.

Part of the future employment problem in our "technological society" may be attributable to the American educational system's limited capacity to respond. One measure of this weakness is the alarming decline in student achievement test scores in mathematics and science in the secondary schools. Moreover, educational opportunities for adults often are limited, of low quality, and unimaginatively structured. Curriculum reform usually is slow—often very slow for lack of resources. The flight of outstanding teachers to better-paying jobs outside of teaching is a serious problem for the secondary schools. Universities are beginning to see symptoms of a similar defection from academe. Fewer students are entering graduate programs in computer science and related fields. Graduate students in those fields are leaving their studies to take jobs, without completing their Ph.D.'s. Faculty have begun to leave academia for industry, as well. It is noteworthy that a recent NSF survey of faculty mobility concluded that salary was not reported as the most compelling reason for leaving academia; several other "institutional disincentives," particularly those affecting research, ranked ahead of salary. We will need to endow our educational system with new resources and imaginative leadership if it is to respond to the crisis suggested by these problems.

Societal attitudes create problems that are more difficult both to measure and to solve. In the 1950's, the British scientist and novelist C. P. Snow described a "gulf of mutual incomprehension" that had opened between scientists and non-scientists. Stanford engineering professor James Adams, who teaches in a program there called "Values, Technology, and Society," put the issue in different terms for *Time* magazine in December, 1982. Said Adams, "The techs (science and engineering) are considered by the fuzzies (liberal arts and humanities) to be nerds. The techs, in turn, consider the fuzzies as only marginal at reaching logical conclusions, probably unable to keep their bicycles in operation and completely unable to support themselves after graduation from college."

Large segments of society outside academia also exhibit nega-tive attitudes toward science and technology, manifesting a type of insecurity that has been labeled "technophobia." So I come to the end of this essay with only one prescription for the good health of employment in America left to share: For all our people, we must find cures for the numerous forms of techno-phobia.

FIVE

The Service Economy and the Changing Job Structures

Eli Ginzberg
Hepburn Professor Emeritus of Economics,
Graduate School of Business
and
Director, Conservation of Human Resources
Columbia University

Eli Ginzberg is Hepburn Professor Emeritus of Economics and Special Lecturer in Business in the Graduate School of Business, Columbia University; Special Lecturer in Health and Society in Barnard College of Columbia; and Director of both the Conservation of Human Resources Project and the Revson Fellows Program for the Future of the City of New York at Columbia University. He is a fellow of the American Academy of Arts and Sciences and a member of the Institute of Medicine of the National Academy of Sciences. He has been a consultant to the Federal Government since 1941 and to major corporations and non-governmental institutions, including DuPont, GE, IBM, AT&T, Celanese, Citicorp, Digital, and the Edna McConnell Clark Foundation, the Ford Foundation, and the Rockefeller Brothers Fund, among others.

Professor Ginzberg served as Chairman of the National Manpower Advisory Committee and the National Commission for Employment Policy from 1962 to 1981. He is Chairman Emeritus of the Board of the Manpower Demonstration Research Corporation.

He has authored more than 60 books, primarily in human resources and manpower, starting with The House of Adam Smith, *which appeared in 1934. His most recent book,* The Large Corporation at Risk: People vs Jobs, *will be published in 1985.*

Introduction

As a researcher who has concentrated on the study of human resources since the late 1930's, I welcome the emphasis that this lecture series has placed on employment and jobs as critical dimensions of the United States economy. The economy and, consequently, employment opportunities have changed profoundly throughout those 40-odd years. Unfortunately, our understanding and appreciation of those changes have not kept pace with the rate of change because, for the most part, we have attempted to explain them in terms of traditional economic models that obscure the very changes that we have tried to study. To better understand our economy and the employment opportunities it creates, then, we must begin by revising our accustomed view of things.

To do this, I will begin by raising some questions about how economists have thought about services in the past, and I will indicate how their conceptualizations must be corrected before we can see our economy as it really is and how it is likely to develop in the future. Then I will set before you a selected number of facts and trends that will highlight the growth of services in the United States economy since the end of World War II, with particular emphasis on the transformation of the labor force and the patterns of employment. I will end by raising a number of policy issues that are embedded in ongoing changes. Although I do not have the answers to all of these issues, I will indicate the directions in which answers can be found.

How Economists Misconceived the Role of Services

Those of you who are acquainted with my bibliography know that I am unlikely to adopt a position critical of Adam Smith who, since I wrote my dissertation, *The House of Adam Smith*, in 1934*, has served as my model of a great economist because of his ability to combine theoretical and institutional analysis and because of his concern with policy. Nevertheless, I ascribe most of

---

* Eli Ginzberg. *The House of Adam Smith* (New York: Columbia University Press, 1934). See in particular Chapter VII.

the flawed treatment of services to my hero, who argued that the test of productive labor was whether it resulted in *physical* output.

The full title of Smith's classic is *An Inquiry into the Nature and Causes of the Wealth of Nations*, which underscored his belief that capital accumulation was the principal element in economic growth. Since he did not consider that the work of the millions of retainers in the great houses of the realm contributed to capital accumulation and growth, he concluded that their service employment was "non-productive." I have more sympathy for Smith's misconception than for its uncritical repetition by his many followers. It would be only a slight exaggeration to claim that contemporary economists still view services as nonproductive, or at least as being of secondary importance. Fuchs, Baumol, and many others are uneasy about the slow gains in productivity that can be achieved in the service sector, but I believe that this is an unwarranted judgment because they ascribe to manufacturing all the gains in efficiency contributed by such services as design, engineering, distribution, finance and other producer services. Long ago, Kuznets warned about these errors of ascription.

Let me provide a less complicated example. In the 1920's, it would have been difficult to imagine that the automotive industry could grow at the rate that it did achieve—a rate that could not have been achieved had it not been for contributions from two related services: the expansion of a strong network of dealers and the recourse to consumer credit. I still recall the head-shaking that occurred on the Columbia campus when my teacher, E.R.A. Seligman, finished his two-volume study for General Motors in which he concluded that there was nothing wrong with buying automobiles and other durable goods on installment.* Parenthetically, the head-shaking related less to his conclusions than to the fact that he received a large honorarium for his study.

Despite the important contributions of the human capital school (Schultz, Becker, Mincer), the American public still is concerned about public investments in services such as education, health, and cultural activities for many of the same reasons that

---

* E. R. A. Seligman, *The Economics of Installment Selling: A Study in Consumers' Credit with Special Reference to the Automobile* (2 vols) (New York: Harper & Bros., 1927).

bothered Smith. Americans still feel that, if the result of public investment does not lead to short-term physical output, there is a strong likelihood that the resources deployed will have been wasted and the nation's wealth will have been diminished. It is worth observing that the Marxist critics of classical political economy, starting with their leader, Karl Marx, succumbed to the same "commodity fetish."

In the late 1960's, the United States State Department expanded its cultural exchange program in the Eastern Bloc countries. To my initial surprise, most of them, from Bulgaria to Czechoslovakia, asked the State Department to send me because they wanted to consult on the role of services. Once I got there, I was less surprised about their request. The absence and poor quality of their services constituted major bottlenecks to their economic development. I found many factories with up-to-date equipment, where the machines were down because of shortcomings in transportation and inventory. They had followed the Marxian precepts and had deliberately curtailed investments in services, which were viewed as "non-productive."

One more illustration of erroneous conceptualization: recently, there has been growing concern with the large trade deficits that the United States has been incurring, especially in the last several years, when the dollar appreciated so greatly in the foreign exchange markets. However, while we have been raking up large deficits in transactions involving goods, we have more than balanced our accounts with gains that we have continued to achieve through the export of services and the earnings on our foreign investments. I am not suggesting that we ignore the sizable gaps that have opened up between our exports and imports of manufactured goods, but that we broaden our perspective to include the growing role that services have come to play in foreign, as well as domestic, economic transactions.

The errors and shortcomings in the ways in which economists think about services can be summarized as follows:

- The distinctions between physical and non-physical output are without merit. To count the manufacture of a piano as productive and a concert by Vladimir Horowitz as non-productive is ridiculous.
- The distinction which economists have made between the produc-

tion and distribution of goods and services is fallacious. It is not true that efficiencies of scale are possible only in the case of goods. (Consider, for example, the economies of scale that have been achieved by chains of hotels, restaurants, auto rental agencies, hospitals, department stores, and the like.) It is equally wrong to hold that services, unlike goods, cannot be transported or exported.

- Much of our confusion about the role of services stems from shortcomings in national income accounting procedures, where, as in the case of banking, inputs are taken as the measure of output. An associated error is the failure to take into account gross changes in quality over time: an appendectomy in 1983 is quite a different procedure (in terms of risk, length of hospital stay, and outcome) than it was 50 years ago.
- The bias of market economists against the expanding role of government has led them to minimize public investments, consisting mostly of services, which are crucial for the continuing vitality of a modern economy.

Most of the foregoing list of misconceptions and errors about services can be traced back to economists' neglect of the dominant role of human resources in economic development.

Facts and Trends in Services and Service Employment

Since the term "services" is used in two different ways, I will define how I deploy the term. In the following analysis, "services" refers to all sectors of the economy other than agriculture, mining, manufacturing, and construction, which are conventionally designated as the "goods sector" to differentiate them from services. Services, in turn, can be categorized as follows: government, nonprofit, mainly consumer, producer, retailing, and distributive. Except in the few instances where measurements in terms of value of output are notably at variance with measurements based on employment data, I will rely primarily on the latter in discussing the principal changes that have occurred in the post-World War II period.

In 1948, after reconversion from the war had been accomplished, services accounted for 55 percent of total employment, while the goods sector accounted for 45 percent. (The United States economy was even then a predominantly service economy.) Current data (1982) reflect a further expansion of services to the point where they now account for slightly over 70 percent of total employment. Edward Denison* has argued that not too much should be made of this shift, which largely reflects a movement of workers out of agriculture into services, since manufacturing, especially in GNP terms, has maintained its relative position. Denison has a point, but, as we shall see, it is not conclusive.

In the 30 years following 1948, manufacturing declined from about 28 percent of GNP to 24 percent. This gives some support to Denison's contention that manufacturing maintained its relative importance in the economy. Nonetheless, if the focus is shifted to the *changes* that occurred during that period, we find that services accounted for about three times more than manufacturing of the total gains in the value of output.

In terms of employment, the gains in services were considerably greater. While employment in manufacturing declined after 1948 from one job in three to slightly more than one in five, the service sector experienced sizable gains in relative, as well as absolute, terms. Over the three decades, the service sector absorbed more than 27 million additional workers, or roughly seven and one-half times the number of jobs added by manufacturing. We can also point out that between 1969 and 1981 total employment, excluding agriculture, increased from 70 to 91 million. During that period of rapid growth in the number of jobs, manufacturing added no workers, while services accounted for all of the job gains with the exception of 1.5 million in mining and construction.

Since services account for so much of the total contemporary economy in terms of both GNP and jobs, it is essential to look more closely at the principal components of the service sector to understand what has been occurring in this highly heterogeneous sector. First, "consumer services" account for less than 3 percent in terms of GNP and less than 5 percent in terms of employment. Clearly, services no longer comprise only dry cleaning establishments, shoe repair shops, laundries, movies, and other consumer

---

* Edward F. Denison, *Accounting for Slower Economic Growth: The United States in the 1970's* (Washington, D. C.: Brookings Institution, 1979).

services. The explosive growth of services has occurred among the following groups: government and retailing, which account for most of the increase; and producer services and non-profit institutions, which, together, contribute sizable gains. The distributive services (transportation, utilities, and wholesaling) experienced relatively slow growth.

Producer services warrant closer inspection. Included in this category are a wide array of activities such as commercial and investment banking, law, accounting, marketing and advertising, communications, management consulting, data processing, and many other enterprises that provide specialized services to profit and nonprofit firms and to government, all of which prefer to purchase rather than provide these critical inputs for themselves. In 1948, producer services accounted for only about 6 percent of all employed workers. Thirty years later its share of employment had doubled and, in terms of GNP, it accounted for just under 20 percent of all output (reflecting the disproportionate number of high earners).

The data presented above refer only to independent firms that provide producer services. During the last three decades, many more services have been produced "in-house" by goods-producing firms. There has been a striking increase in the proportion of workers in United States manufacturing concerns who are not directly engaged in production. In a classic manufacturing firm, such as General Electric, an informed estimate suggests that not more than 35 percent of all employees are directly involved in manufacturing. If the concept of producer services is broadened to encompass both in-house and independent firms, the net value added at least would equal, and probably would exceed, that of all manufacturing!

Let us consider briefly the role of producer services in two cities: New York and Nashville, Tennessee. In New York City, six out of seven jobs currently are in the services sector. Two producer services, law and air transportation, account for the largest value added in the export sector and are more important in this respect than New York City's two principal manufacturing industries, garment and printing. Much the same is true of Nashville, with its financial institutions, insurance companies, hospital chains, governmental agencies, educational institutions, and tourist industry, major components of which represent producer services.

It is important to note the underlying forces that are drawing the United States and other advanced economies more and more into services:

- As my colleagues, Thomas Stanback and Thierry Noyelle, constantly remind me, it is not only *what* we produce but *how* we produce that is being radically altered. Consider agriculture, where the effective full-time labor force has been reduced to about 2 million. In the process of reducing the number of farm workers, we have come to rely increasingly on airplanes for seeding and pest control; on trucks and railroads for shipping large quantities of fuel to the farm to power ever more complex machinery, which also requires repair and maintenance; and on schools for ultimately replacing illiterate farm hands with managers who hold master's degrees and who use computers to decide what to plant and when and where to sell what is grown.
- The consuming public has demonstrated a clear preference for novelty, quality, and convenience, and this has been reflected in more emphasis on design, engineering, specialty shops and boutiques, and other marketing innovations.
- The computer has contributed to vast improvements in the quality of information and to the speed with which critical information is processed. In turn, this is transforming more and more of the economy, including such important sectors as financial institutions, manufacturing (CAD-CAM), distribution (inventory control and reorders), travel, and much more.
- The computer surely has been a precondition for the rise of large service companies that range from ITT to McDonald's to the Hilton hotel chain.
- Undergirding all of the foregoing has been the steady rise in the quality of the nation's human resources, which has resulted from significant improvements in their education, health, and standard of living and has provided the spur to the growth of services. These improvements have altered the way in which people prepare for work and ultimately perform their work.

Changes in the Work Force and Work

Let us briefly consider each in turn. The quality of the nation's pool of human resources has undergone striking improvements over my lifetime. When I graduated from college in 1931, the proportion of my age group who acquired baccalaureate degrees was in the range of 4 to 5 percent; today it is close to 30 percent. A half century ago, most young people entering the labor force had completed one or two years of high school; today the average is one year of post-secondary education. In World War II, rejection rates for educational deficiency (which were defined as fewer than five years of schooling) exceeded, in several Southern states, 60 per 1000 white registrants and over 200 per 1000 non-whites—a sorry record indeed for a nation that had been in the forefront of public education. Today, the large majority of whites and blacks, 90 and 80 percent respectively, complete high school.

For the first time in the nation's history, the number of women enrolled in college is greater than the number of men. Moreover, there have been striking increases in the proportion of blacks who are enrolled in, and who subsequently graduate from, college. Between 1960 and 1981, the percentage of white high school graduates enrolled in college increased from 24.2 to 32.5 percent while the percentage for black high school graduates increased from 18.4 to 28 percent.

While discrimination against women and blacks in the labor market surely has not been eliminated, it has been substantially reduced in the last several decades, as each group has made sizable gains in entering and advancing into professional and technical and managerial and administrative jobs—the two job categories that are at the top of the hierarchy of earning and prestige. It is hard to believe that when I wrote *The Negro Potential* in 1956*, I could find black men employed in manufacturing jobs in the South only in sawmills and in steel mills, where they worked as furnace operators.

We can mention briefly other breakthroughs: the much enlarged participation of women in the labor force (from less than one-third of the work force in the late 1940's to over half today); the explosion in white-collar employment; and the rapid increase in the number of professional and technical jobs, which grew from 7 million to over 14 million in the last 20 years. The growth observed in professional, technical, and other white-

---

* Eli Ginzberg with the assistance of James K. Anderson, Douglas W. Bray, and Robert W. Smuts, *The Negro Potential* (New York: Columbia University Press, 1956).

collar jobs is linked directly to the expansion of services and to increased employment of women.

A few observations are also in order about the changes that have been occurring in the ways in which people prepare for work and subsequently perform their work. As indicated by the figures, contemporary Americans spend a greater amount of time in preparation for work than did their predecessors, but they also spend a much longer time in retirement. For every year that they spend preparing for work or in retirement, they will spend approximately one year in the labor force.

Many service jobs do not require employees to work a full day or a five-day week. Many employees, especially married women, students and older workers, prefer less than full-time employment. Small wonder, therefore, that of all people who work during the course of a year, about 45 percent work less than full time or less than a full year, which has been and remains the dominant pattern in manufacturing, particularly in durable goods manufacturing.

One of the difficulties encountered in assessing a service economy is that of determining work norms for jobs in which much of the employee's activity consists of oral and written communication and where the employee's goal is, or should be, closely linked to *quality*. Hours worked is a poor measure of productivity and a piece-work standard frequently is impractical. One wants to judge teachers, not by the number of pupils in their classes, but according to what their pupils learn and retain. Much the same is apparent in assessing the productivity of physicians. There is little point in their seeing more patients if they fail to diagnose correctly many of those whom they see. Similarly, expensive restaurants pride themselves on the manner in which their staff interacts with the clientele; the services of many retail outlets depend on the interest, skill, and commitment of their sales forces.

Since quality, which dominates a service economy, is so difficult to control and even more difficult to measure, I suspect that some of our recent handwringing over the low productivity of American workers may be linked to faulty accounting, as the economy increasingly shifts to services.

This suspicion is heightened by what many of us believe to be a steady increase in the off-the-record economy, which also is linked directly to the growth of services. It is difficult for a manufacturer of dresses to exchange them with a manufacturer of lamps or fountain pens. But it is relatively easy for a dentist and a tax accountant to exchange their services, which then are not included directly on either the output or the expenditure side of the national income accounts. As one moves from the direct exchange of services to illicit and illegal transactions, the accounting problems mount. Some of the most knowledgeable students believe that off-the-record transactions are equal to 10 percent of GNP, a considerable figure since ours is a $3 trillion plus economy.

Changing contours of the work force and the work associated with the expansion of services include:

- The continuing increases in total employment.
- The substantially enlarged participation of women and minorities in the labor force.
- The significant upgrading in the quality of the labor force.
- The shift from blue-collar to white-collar jobs, with the most rapid expansion occurring at the top, in professional and technical positions.
- The high proportion of workers who are employed less than full time or less than a full year.
- The growing proportion of the life span that people devote to preparing for work or spend in retirement.
- The uncertain, but probably substantial, growth of the off-the-record economy.

Many analysts, including my colleagues at Columbia, would add one additional observation: a bifurcation between high-paying and low-paying service jobs, which contrast to the more regular progression in manufacturing from poor jobs to good ones. It may be that this is an illusion—that manufacturing employees can advance within the large plant where they first went to work while service workers change employers frequently to better themselves.

Policy Directions

It is likely that manufacturing will go the way of agriculture; that is, that it will require fewer and fewer unskilled and semi-skilled workers and rely increasingly on large inputs of capital and sophisticated human resources. But changes in technology are intertwined with changes in trade patterns, of which accelerating internationalization is the single most striking development. Some analysts believe that the microprocessor will result in a downscaling of plants, which will facilitate their better adaptation to local and regional markets along the lines of the smaller specialty steel plants. But we must wait and see. Detroit's reach to install robots speaks to the survival of large manufacturing units.

The foregoing analysis points to several other policy issues. First, it implicitly challenges those who advocate the "reindustrialization" of the United States economy. This challenge, of course, does not carry the implication that we can be indifferent to whether our steel industry survives, if only in reduced scale. Next, it should offer some support to those who do not believe that further declines in manufacturing employment will lead to a national crisis, however difficult such a decline is likely to be for many of the dislocated workers. Finally, it reminds us that, with agriculture as a model, we can remain a powerful exporter even though only 2 to 3 percent of the labor force remains attached to a major sector.

Since most young people today graduate from high school and a high proportion go on to college, the United States cannot look forward in the years ahead to a large increase in the quality of the labor pool comparable to the increase in quality that was experienced in the past three decades. The best prospects for improving our human resources will be to raise the quality of instruction in our secondary schools, many of which currently fail to do a good, or even adequate, job in teaching the basics.

Second, we must broaden the scope, scale, and depth of continuing education and training beyond the sizable efforts already underway in industry and in the community.

Special attention must be directed to the sizable cohort of students who, with a marked overrepresentation of minority groups, drop out of high school without having acquired a reasonable level of functional literacy; that is, 9th to 10th grade competence. There is less and less room for such poorly educated persons to make their way in a service economy and almost no way for them to move into good jobs. The major challenge must be to raise the performance capabilities of inner-city public schools.

A service economy is heavily dependent on constant additions to the pool of knowledge, which can serve as the foundation for new industries. There is no simple, or even complex, way to decide how much of private and public investment should be funneled into research and development, but it is essential that an advanced economy not skimp in this regard. With the Federal budget under severe constraints, with many industries lacking traditions of such investments, and with even our most distinguished research universities unable to purchase up-to-date equipment, there is a real danger that our nation may be underinvesting in our future.

A related problem recently has surfaced. Because of low salaries and poor equipment, many engineering schools are losing critical faculty to business, with serious consequences for the future supply of engineers. Corrective action, in the form of large private donations from science-based companies, has begun to address the issue, though the resource imbalance is not likely to be corrected without significant state and federal funding.

The engineering manpower issue is complicated by the fact that, 15 years after graduation, about two-thirds of all engineers have left the field for related assignments, primarily in sales and management. Moreover, most companies have been unwilling to make the substantial investments in continuing education without which young engineers lose their edge or become so specialized that the possibility of their reassignment becomes more and more constrained.

In formulating national policy, including tax and trade policy, both the executive and the legislative branches have been unduly influenced by the manufacturing model. Lately, both the Administration and the Congress have become more aware of the growing importance of services, in part because of the new consortium of leading service companies that has sought to inform the public about the extent to which the United States economy is dominated by services. Nevertheless, the relative neglect by academicians, policy analysts, and politicians of the role of services and the means with which to strengthen them will not be remedied quickly, even if the information drive continues. We need to broaden and deepen our understanding of the workings of the service economy so that policy initiatives to speed its development will succeed.

I noted earlier that strong job creation was one of the favorable concomitants of the growth of the service economy, even though many of the service jobs are not full-time and do not pay much above the minimum wage. I also noted that young people who do not acquire functional literacy are at a severe disadvantage in their attempts to obtain and retain employment. The recent, prolonged recession, particularly in durable goods manufacturing—which may be followed by significant job losses among white-collar personnel as the computer-communications revolution gains strength—points to the desirability, at least to me, if not to the President and his advisors, of putting a Federal job creation program in place to assure that large numbers of structurally unemployed persons are not ejected from the economy and subsequently alienated from society. I grant that an effective program is difficult to design and even more difficult to run, but even an imperfect job program is better than widespread frustration and discontent, the likely byproducts of idleness that can undermine the fabric of a democratic society. We have had good experience during the past third of a century in expanding service jobs in all three sectors—profit, nonprofit, and government. In the period ahead—let us hope that it will be less than a third of a century—we will need a Federal job program to absorb many who are being victimized by the dynamics of the economy. What is there to fear? As FDR remarked, we have nothing to fear but fear itself.

SIX

Current Conceptions of Unemployment: Some Logical and Empirical Difficulties

Ivar Berg
Associate Dean for Undergraduate Studies
School of Arts and Sciences
University of Pennsylvania

Ivar Berg is Associate Dean for Undergraduate Studies, School of Arts and Sciences, at the University of Pennsylvania. He studied at Colgate University, the University of Oslo, and Harvard University, where he was awarded the Ph.D. in sociology. He is a member of Phi Beta Kappa and Beta Gamma Sigma, and is a fellow of the American Association for the Advancement of Science. He is a former Fulbright Scholar, and has received the National Woodrow Wilson Fellowship, the Chester Hastings Arnold Fellowship in Contemporary Civilization, the National Institute of Mental Health Fellowship, a Guggenheim Fellowship, and the Rockefeller Fellowship in the Humanities.

Professor Berg has consulted with a variety of firms and agencies, including AT&T, IBM, Western Electric, the Department of Labor, the Russell Sage Foundation, the National Institute of Mental Health, and others. He is a prolific contributor to his field. Education and Jobs: The Great Training Robbery, *which was published in 1970, was named "One of the Ten Most Important Books" in the field of industrial relations by the Princeton University Industrial Relations Section in 1971.*

Note: This paper was originally prepared for the ITT Key Lecture Series, for presentation at Vanderbilt University in January, 1983. It is a revised version of the ITT lecture prepared for a forthcoming volume edited by Arthur P. Brief and Johannes M. Pennings, *Productivity Research in the Behavioral and Social Sciences* (New York: Praeger, 1984).

Introduction

Studies in the post World War II period of the workaday experiences of Americans have been dominated by social science investigators, both liberal and conservative, who share in the assumption that employers are economic rationalists who simply "do" in the labor market, as in other markets in which they engage in transactions, "what they have to do." Employers, in these investigations seek to minimize risks, minimize the costs of resources (including information costs), combine the factors of production in optimally profitable ways, and plan their operations with an eye to both short-term gains and such longer-term ends as growth or stability.

As Marxists see things, employers hope for labor redundancies—what they term a surplus army of labor—and seek to maximize and then to appropriate the so-called surplus value generated by workers. As employers see it, workers' own urges to aggrandize are best tempered by circumstances assuring that there are adequate numbers of competitors among the ranks of their unemployed peers.

Keynesians, and not a few of those given to the most notable alternative view among social science orthodoxies, who debate about public economic policy interventions, have modernized the Marxist model slightly. Their aim, however, has not been to purify Marxism of its errors, but to pinpoint the size and composition of the surpluses in labor markets needed to achieve the best possible balance between unemployment and inflation rates; they have, however, done the Marxist model, in this particular event, surprisingly little damage.

In these debates, employers' preferences for one or another admixture of productive resources are universally conceded, though implicitly for the most part, to be rational ones whose measures may be taken collectively, by published information on wage rates, hires, discharges, layoffs, training investments, capital purchases, and so on. According to the theory (which remarkably both postulates and affirms the consequent), competitive forces will eventually drive employers to behave, in their purchases and in their own pricing practices, in precisely those ways that are subsequently reflected "in the numbers." There is no need, here, to rehearse the details of this generic theme in the model's variant forms. It is sufficient, at this point, simply to note that in our discussion of unemployment, we do not, most of us, stray far apart in our conceptualization of what employers do (or why they do it) when it comes to their acquisitions and deployments of human resources and their payments thereto.

Of immediate concern to me are the specific problems in dealing with unemployment that derive, in straightforward terms, from the very widely held assumption that employers are essentially passive actors in unfolding labor market dramas.[1] As I see it, this assumption—I may call it the theodicy of innocence—leads us, more unwittingly than otherwise, to constrain our conceptualizations, to limit our selections of research methods, to beg a number of strategic issues, to gainsay a great deal of relevant evidence, and to virtually misspecify the terms in our equations having to do with labor supply and the demand for labor. The result of the theodicy is to compound the difficulties we confront, otherwise, in efforts to discuss economic policy questions with an eye to realism.

I will *not* assert that our conventional efforts in unemployment studies are totally wrong, in the most fundamental sense of the phrase. Rather, I would like to suggest that most of the variants of the conventional model, whatever their particular ideological-partisan slants, fail to obey Max Weber's wonderfully apt dictum that partisans' biases often prevent them from tripping over inconvenient facts, but that "... for *every* partisan opinion there are facts that are extremely inconvenient."

My central proposition is that we too often confound "the structure of unemployment" with "structural unemployment." We thereby enhance our confidence in a model rather more than we deepen our understanding of the problem to which we seek to fit and apply the model. After we test this proposition against the theodicy of innocence, in the initial section of the paper, we can identify some additional propositions about the problem in the

---

[1]Even Marx, after admitting that he, in no sense, "painted the capitalist *en couleur de rose*," absolved the capitalist of malevolent urges, claiming that he was more concerned with the "locomotive forces" at work in capitalist systems that forced employers to act as they do. In the modern version of this mechanistic Cartesian metaphor, tastes, preferences, and propensities, otherwise unspecified, are attributed to employers from the mountains of data as the empirical results of rational economic decisions, whatever might have really motivated the actors.

so-called structural unemployment thesis, move to propositions about "correctives" that might add to the conventional model's analytical power, and finally, to a very few concluding remarks.

The "Structure of Unemployment" and "Structural Unemployment"

Most Americans date the education boom in the 1960's with the successful launching of Sputnik by the Soviets, but most social scientists, joined by many of their academic colleagues otherwise, will give abundant credit for the sustained quality of the boom to reports by economists, in the very early 1960's, of: (1) the contributions of educational investments, net of other investments, to the economic growth rates of the industrial nations; and (2) of the cognate roles played by differential educational achievements, net of their other attributes, in the distribution of Americans' earnings. During that period, much was also offered in the mass (and other) media of the skirmishes against the academic shortcomings of the poor—shortcomings that the strategists in the War Against Poverty fought hard to correct.

These studies of economic growth and income distribution by "human capital" and "status attainment" investigators underwrote the conclusion that most low-paid and unemployed workers, had they been better educated, would have been better off in an economy in which the emerging occupational structure favored those with more years of schooling. In view of these studies' results, many of the strategic weapons that might have been deployed in battles against poverty were gradually abandoned in favor of tactical weapons. The "war against poverty" remained a policy aim, to be sure. Nonetheless, the most energetic maneuvers in the war focused on the obstacles that blocked the prospects for poor people obtaining the "human capital" wherewithal that, according to investigators' reports, were prerequisite to the legitimation, in technical terms, of "have littles' " and "have nots' " claims to better jobs.

In the strictest sense, the tactics worked. Where, in 1960, the two highest-ability quartiles of the lowest-income sons' and daughters' probabilities of entering college, for example, were .25 and .48, for men, respectively, and .18 and .34, for women, respectively, improvements occurred such that by 1972 no less than 64 percent of all the highest-ability high school graduates from the poorest-income quartile were enrolled in post-secondary schools. The educational gains for the able "have nots" in a 12-year period were truly remarkable, no doubt about it. The gains of individual black income earners, as against those of white, holding education constant, however, have not been anywhere near as great.

The argument that the occupational structure (for all the admitted increases in demands for professional, managerial, and technical personnel from 1945 to 1965) really *required* all the educational achievements we were encouraging beyond 1965 was essentially based on an assumption that is not as readily tested as one would wish. The assumption was that the high and positive correlations between education and income in economists' and sociologists' reports simply reflected differences in the productivity of differentially educated workers: better-educated people earned more than their less-educated peers in virtue of their being proportionately more productive.

My own investigations into the matter, though less elegantly simple than those to which I have alluded, were "direct" rather than "indirect:" I sought to test, though it could only be done crudely, this widely assumed causal relationship between education and productivity, leaving income aside. My efforts involved imprecise measures, reflecting the almost incredible difficulties—odd, considering the widespread belief in the productivity assumption—in measuring the productivity of individuals.

My results strongly suggested, at least, that the basic inferences about education and productivity on which policies increasingly came to rest were, at the very least, problematic ones:[2] I observed no differences in their job performance among differentially educated scientists and engineers; textile workers; telephone installers; a news magazine's editorial assistants; a "high tech" company's managers; Prudential's salesmen; commissioned sailors, airmen, soldiers, and marines; and technicians in a chemical company, among others. All the comparisons were

---

[2]For a discussion, see Ivar Berg, *Education and Jobs: The Great Training Robbery* (New York: Praeger, 1970).

made of workers doing the same work or, in the case of military personnel, taking the same formal training courses.

The problematic character of assumptions about productivity underlying investigations of education's contribution to individuals or society has rarely stopped us, however, from acting in policy and other realms as if they are essentially valid. And many of us, quite understandably, have vested interests in the "as ifs" postulated by the marginalists among us. In addition to being marginalists, we are members of the academic community; as such we have no small interests in studies purporting to show that social and private investments in our schools, colleges, and universities (and in educators) are especially among those to which handsome social returns will accrue; indeed, the conceits of a community have not enjoyed as much empirical support since the Pharisees, in defense of their piety, took attendance at temple.

A few of us, as my own study suggested, were skeptical of our applications of our marginalist assumptions. It was our suspicion that both popular beliefs and public policies holding that persons with more schooling are paid more because they are more productive were organized around several sets of empirical studies whose interpretations were informed by a tautology: better-educated people are paid more because they are proportionately more productive than their less-educated peers. How do we know so? We are assured of their higher productivity precisely because they are better paid! In the event, some of us suggested, we might be confusing our *explanans* with our *explanandum* not less than we were confounding our *difiens* with our *difiendum*.

These suspicions, having been documented in 1970, gained strength as time passed and further studies were completed. Thus, we learned that private rates of returns to education in the 1970's were beginning to decline. Richard Freeman, the author of the first major empirical study of the turnabout, on a more Philistine than Pharisaical note, entitled his work *The Overeducated Americans*.³ It is not the least evident that it occurred to Professor Freeman, while performing his research in the mid-1970's on private returns to educational investments, that some of the higher returns to educational investments, in what my

---

³R. B. Freeman, *The Overeducated American:* (New York: Academic Press, 1976).

colleague and fellow contributor to this volume, Prof. Michael Wachter, terms the halcyon days of the 1950's and 1960's, might effectively have been handouts from managers who did not know better than to pay excessive wages and salaries to well-educated workers;[4] or, more likely, that they were the handouts of employers whose firms operated in less than fully competitive markets and who could, for a time, ignore some costs; or, conceivably, that the productivity of the nation's teachers and professors had declined in the amount of the reduced returns accorded their graduates. It is, realistically speaking, almost impossible to gainsay the notion that some combination of these possibilities explains some of the changes reported in Freeman's study.

Neither was Professor Freeman prepared to make the motion that we repeal the law of supply and demand, though his evidence led me, as I read along, to expect that he might do so as he wound down to the end of his report. All was going along well, he implies, in the *earlier* period. "And then, in the 1970's," he notes in his dust jacket blurb, "something went wrong." The evolution from pharisaical illogic to the hypocrisies of Philistines ends up with the casuistry of Sophists: when education is better rewarded, empirically, it is because it was a valuable factor of production on the supply side; when it is not so well rewarded, it is because employers' demand for education has declined.

Like Professor Freeman, many of us wanted it both ways: if the parameters of one's dependent variable are no longer to be conveniently (i.e. tautologically) converted into its own explanation, because the parameters have changed, then we don't go back to re-examine the earlier model; we construct an additional model, use the two models at different times, letting events dictate to us which model is to be used, and imply that we can bypass the education-productivity connection in the first model when we substitute the second one. Unaddressed in this assessment is the possibility that rewards for education were as

---

[4]Owen D. Young, the great industrialist-statesman, once remarked that, "It is not the crook we need fear in modern business but the honest businessman who does not know what he is doing." I overheard a Vanderbilt colleague, responding to a business executive (after a lecture on price theory) who protested that neither he nor one of his associates had ever plotted the intercepts of any marginal cost with marginal revenue curves, "Yes you have, without knowing it and—besides—in the aggregate the [relevant theory] fits the facts very nicely."

high as they were, in the halcyon days, not for reasons related to education's productivity but to market imperfections that allowed employers to act whimsically.

The facts, we seem to say, may be represented by numbers in continuous time series but the explanations thereof can be accommodated to theory by the convenient expedient of splitting the theory in two: one for demand, for our Monday, Wednesday and Friday classes, and another, for supply, for Tuesday, Thursday, Saturday class sessions. Nor are the contradictions, I suggest, fully resolved for most of us in the academy, in Sunday reflections by academics that link the decline in the educational returns to our former students to declines in our own real incomes. I commend this exercise, however; now that our real wages in the academy have gone down, we might conclude that we are less productive in our contributions to human capital formation nowadays than during the halcyon days. The labor supply model, after all, explains, by extension, our earning growth in the 1960's as a reward for our productivity.

The so-called human capital paradigm has "stood the test" of uncritical reviews somewhat better than the tests of either time or the skeptics' empirically supported grounds for urging revisions in its specifications.

We should point out that the earliest version of a labor supply theory, its concerns, at the time, about the youth cohort's size fairly well muted, was seized upon by liberals who were sympathetic toward unemployed youths, their families, and their communities and, not least, to the disadvantaged ethnic groups from which they came. The solutions that they favored in the halcyon days were embodied, as Professor Johnson points out elsewhere in these pages, in five "waves" of job training programs. These programs were conceived as the instruments by which work-willing but deficient youths could become "employable."

However, the theodicy of innocence—a theodicy that explains the ways of management in totally mechanistic terms—makes much less of youth's ingenuousness; where there are innocent employers there are, by implications, guilty parties elsewhere to be found. Accordingly, for years, some of us implicitly damned the unemployed for their unresponsiveness to opportunities to enter the innumerable "dead end" jobs, especially in the service sector, deplored their fanciful expectations, mocked their willingness to accept welfare-type supports (which until recently, as Professor Wachter notes, reduced the costs of unemployment and thus the interests of the unemployed in seeking jobs), and, otherwise, bemoaned youth's nutant spirits.

If many of us were taken with the human capital phase of the labor supply theory's evolution, our ranks have been swollen significantly by admirers of the work by a second generation of labor supply theorists in which the theodicy of innocence has been augmented by an additional teleological proof. As the labor supply model has evolved, however, the implicit charges of guilt have been levelled at targets even farther removed from employers than the youths they do not hire. In the augmented version, the persons implicitly arraigned for the economic injustices recently visited upon youths are the parents, less continent than they were speculative, who delivered unto us the so-called baby boom.[5]

The new addition to the labor supply model, more explicitly demographic in its method, is especially interesting because it seeks, in its emphasis on flows on the supply side of labor market transactions, to pick up where the human capital portion of the labor supply thesis has its limits. Newer labor market entrants, according to the revisionists, suffer in these transactions not only because they are relatively inexperienced, which has always been a factor in their earnings, but all the more so, since the early 1960's, because the baby boom's members entered the market in such large numbers that they crowded each other out.

Professor Michael Wachter thus suggests elsewhere in this volume that there are limits, at any given point in an industrial society's development, on the extent to which employers *can* substitute lower wage, unskilled inexperienced help for more skilled and experienced workers. These limits are most generally seen to be given by firms' production methods, the state of their

---

[5]See R. A. Easterlin, M. L. Wachter, and S. M. Wachter, "The Changing Impact of Population Swings on the American Economy" in *Proceedings of the American Philosophical Society*, Vol. 122, No. 3, (June 1978), pp. 119–130, for an analysis of the baby boom holding that "the initiation of these population movements is due to independent or exogenous developments in aggregate demand, typically a private investment boom." (p. 213)

technologies, and the divisions of labor and skill hierarchies that derive therefrom.

In some instances, as where collective bargaining agreements obtain, there may be additional limits on employers' unilateral capacities to deploy human resources through contractually agreed upon "work rules" governing job ladders, crew sizes, and skill "jurisdiction." Since youths, especially, cannot adjust readily to forces over which, after all, they have little control, they are others' victims. They also victimize each other, in a sense, because of the size of their so-called cohort. While Professor Wachter himself makes very little of technological change in this process, a point on which, as we will see, I am in full agreement, many of his fellow theorists would add that these changes cause additional "structural" problems for youths and re-entering women.

According to the most Cartesian, least moralistic version of the theodicy of innocence, we must, for a time, write off many of the unemployed (whose services, given minimum wage laws, our curve-crossing employers cannot afford to pay) as the unfortunate soldiers whose sacrifices are needed, though without combat pay, in the battle against renewed inflation. Our consolation, as Professor Wachter points out in his lecture, more or less, lies in the fact that the baby boom cohort's successor group, the baby bust cohort, is reaching labor market entry age in numbers far more in line with employers' demands for neophytes than they were in the legion ahead of them.

The theodicy of innocence is clearly not totally devoid of merit. Nor can it be denied that some of our manpower programs in the 1960's and 1970's often were pro rather than contra-cyclical because they came "on stream" too late to be serviceable. Finally, it cannot be denied that many of the beneficiaries, while unemployed, were not poor, as both Professors Wachter and Johnson point out. Neither can it be simply gainsaid that there are *some* problems incident to the matter of labor market age cohort members' intergroup substitutability.

As the tone of the foregoing commentary may suggest, however, I feel that there are some problems in the formulations according simple and essentially sovereign theoretical primacy to factors linked to the attributes of population segment, their size, or a combination thereof, in explaining their fates, individually or collectively. Reasons for skepticism, I suggest, are rooted in the fact that the second phase of the labor supply modelling involves an extension of the tautology in the first phase's premises. Thus many of us argued, in the 1960's and 1970's, that better educated workers were better paid because they were more productive; the evidence of their productivity being their incomes. Now, we argue, the largest demographic group in the ranks of the unemployed suffers its fate because it is a large, relatively unproductive cohort, the evidence of the cohort's deficient productivity residing in its unemployment rates!

Let us pause here to note the possibility, at least, of some confusion. Consider that when we speak of "the structure of unemployment" we speak of the traits of the unemployed, most especially their demographic and human capital traits. When we speak of "structural unemployment" we imply that we are speaking about a large number of realities of the economy—employers' differential demands for skills, especially. In the revised labor supply approach, with its emphases on the experience and educational achievement of cohorts of different sizes, we transmogrify the *demographic* traits of the unemployed, "the structure of unemployment," into a description of the economic structures that confront them as they seek jobs; their demographic traits thereby become the explanations for their unhappy circumstances. Our newest contribution to our understanding of youth employment, thus, comes disconcertingly close to the nominalism in our earlier contribution.

In this section we have identified some problems of an essentially logical character, problems that invite some skepticism, at least, about the labor supply-human capital-cohort crowding thesis. In the next section we turn to several methodological and empirical problems with which we must also come to terms.

Problems for the Structural Unemployment Thesis

As we have noted, the structural unemployment and labor supply theses make a great deal, in causal terms, of the characteristics of the bulk of our unemployed, focusing on what are taken to be their deficient training, experiences, formal educations, and work attitudes[6], and the cohort size of their larger population components. In the view of the thesis' proponents, these traits, by and large, leave the unemployed workers appreciably and thus understandably less attractive to employers.

Even when they look at the unemployed in longitudinal terms, many labor supply theorists generally restrict their analyses to aggregated data and (with Professor Wachter an admirable exception) assign considerable weight to the role of technological change. They also make a number of assumptions about the understandings new workers have about the labor market, about the ways in which employers locate job candidates, and about the ways in which employers hire workers. Many of them also assume that employers pay wages for and, in strict economic terms, rationally utilize the educational and training achievements of those they employ. They infer, from the relatively higher quit rates of youths in published data on the unemployed, that the instability of their work experiences contributes, in a self-defeating fashion, to the unemployed workers' difficulties. Some of them, like Professor Wachter, I would suggest, exaggerate the voluntariness of youth unemployment, by pooling "quits" with "new entrants" and "re-entrants," to reach a voluntary unemployment figure for youths of 60 percent! Many also assume that among the unemployed group, there is a very large "hard core," like a "hard core" poverty population, whose socially unattractive ways and means confound public policy initiatives, though a few, including Professor Wachter, recognize that a large majority of unemployed youths are in this status for remarkably short periods. Finally, they accept, in all essential ways, the notion that there is an inevitable and calculable trade-off between wage inflation and unemployment rates. These trade-offs can be plotted, in the fashion of Phillips Curves, when annual unemployment rates are cross-tabulated with the annual rates of wage inflation. When declining unemployment rates reach a point at which labor markets become "too tight," according to the theory,

---

[6]Not all labor supply writers fault the attitudes of unemployed youths. Professor Wachter, in his writings, is not persuaded that the unemployed do not want to work. He does, however, make a great deal of the degree to which youth unemployment reflects a protracted period, now over, when the costs to them of youths' unemployment, due to welfare-type arrangements, were too low.

these *rates* literally *cause* inflation. Demographic profiles not only bespeak causes, they become causes. Measures become indicators and indicators become variables that are independent or dependent in a theory that initially affirms what it sets out to prove. There thus exists an "unemployment equilibrium" point and it *defines* the moment when the economy is alternately too overheated or sufficiently cooled for inflation to wax or wane.

I would like to suggest, in the rest of this section, that there are nine reasons for urging that we pronounce, at least temporarily, the Scottish verdict of "not proved" on the newer, updated version of the labor supply thesis.

First off, many of us have vivid memories of World War II, during which we met an explosive demand for human resources to perform hundreds of thousands of jobs for which only very small numbers, in any even remotely meaningful sense, had been either educated or trained to perform. And we met extraordinarily differentiated demands, overnight, with astounding success. I might add that by no means all of the nation's output in these hectic years was produced by employers protected against the putatively low productivity of inefficient and inexperienced work crews by their ability to charge off unacceptably high marginal costs in "cost-plus" government contracts; such contracts affected relatively few employment settings. Nor is it true that wage controls were terribly effective across the board; then as during the period in which President Nixon followed an "incomes policy," *many* workers' job titles could be changed; their wages and salaries could then exceed legally-fixed limits and be justified as incidental to promotions.

In research terms, we may think of World War II as a strategically important "critical experiment," a single but very revealing occurrence. In company with 10 classmates from low-income families in the early 1940's, all of us with unpromising academic records, for example, I became a semi-skilled printer—stocking, feeding, inking, operating, and adjusting three different and mammoth multi-color presses—in six weeks of part-time high school work during my sophomore year.

The detailed labor market developments occurring during World War II have, however, been essentially gainsaid by nearly every one of us in the social sciences who has written on problems in labor economics. The utilization we made of our human resources in the early part of that six-year period, meanwhile, does not fit at all well the models we currently construct. Nor can patriotism and fears of losing a war, by themselves, *magically* convert a generation of teenagers into skilled, useful workers and literally millions of workers-in-uniform; the most laudable of motives are not worth much without operable equipment; *truly* rational, technically well-equipped, and inspired employers; attractive wages; and the availability of jobs.

Second, the concentration in the favored thesis on the flawed attributes shared by large numbers of the unemployed can easily blind us to the experiences of the large numbers among Americans currently *employed*, who clearly share most of the attributes of their unemployed peers. Indeed, though we overlook the inconvenient fact, the majority of labor force participants with the most modest human capital traits are employed! We will return to this issue below, pausing here to note only that there is, overall, as much variation in the educational achievements of those *within* almost all occupations as there is *between* those of workers in the majority of all American occupations.[7]

Third, let us consider the role of technological changes on the tasks performed by millions of Americans. As Fitoussi and Georgescu-Roegen have recently pointed out, "novelty," including novel technology, clearly is a major factor in all industrial economies.[8] But there is no demonstrable evidence, as Professor Wachter allows, that these changes have significant effects on the specific demands for the most notable of the human capital attributes stressed in the conventional wisdom. Consider that the last really thoroughgoing study of the subject concluded that technical changes can double the product of an hour's work in 24 years. The time scale of technological change has, indeed, been shrinking, but the *feeling*, among many analysts, that there are revolutionary technological changes abroad in our economy is not the same as real revolutionary change; while 24 years is perhaps only half a working life time, it *is*, after all, a relatively long time. Survey respondents agree: a scant 2.5 percent of 2,622 member

---

[7]For a discussion see I. Berg, *op. cit.*

[8]Jean-Paul Fitoussi and Nicholas Georgescu-Roegen, "Structure and Involuntary Unemployment," in Edmond Malinuard and Jean-Paul Fitoussi, *Unemployment in Western Countries* (London: Macmillan, 1980), pp. 206–227.

probability sample of all employed Americans reported to Ann Arbor investigators that their jobs "had changed significantly" during a one-year period; most of those changes were organizational, not technical, in character. Other studies also suggest that technological challenges be viewed with drier eyes.[9]

To his credit, Professor Wachter, a structural employment thesis stalwart, reminded his Vanderbilt University audience that the biggest currently heralded bugaboos, computers, are becoming smaller, less complex, and easier to operate; it is quite likely, he argues, that these devices will be used by employers with an eye to the labor skills they will need to hire.

The social science literature on workers and managers, finally, is almost unimaginably crowded with studies of their inventive adaptations to change in work methods, with little or no fuss apart from the need to renegotiate work rules and the need to afford workers in the "internal labor markets" some training on the job.[10]

Fourth, I would like to suggest that the best available evidence about the work-related attitudes of American youths is far more redeeming of them than is commonly supposed by many labor supply theorists. Leonard Goodwin has shown, for example, that attitudes toward employment of low-income female household heads, in company with those of their teenage children, deteriorated precisely as their labor market encounters would suggest: such attitudes go from hopeful optimism to despair as the parents (and the offspring) in the sample move through one unpromising job after another, including pauses for progressively less eager but apparently attentive participation in one or another training program.[11]

Michael Piore reminds us that the jobs of high-unemployment groups pay low wages, are often menial in content, require trivial skills, occur most frequently in troubled industries, are especially vulnerable to sudden shifts in consumer tastes, are in marginal

---

[9]See Ivar Berg, *Industrial Sociology* (Englewood Cliffs, N.J.: Prentice-Hall, 1979), pp. 68–72.

[10]See relevant references and case study materials presented in Peter Doeringer and Michael Piore, *Internal Labor Markets and Manpower Analysis.* (Lexington, Mass.: Heath, 1960) and Michael Piore, "The Impact of Labor Market Upon the Design and Selection of Productive Techniques Within the Manufacturing Plant," *Quarterly Journal of Economics* 82 (November 1968), 602–620.

[11]Leonard Goodwin, *Do the Poor Want to Work? A Social-Psychological Study of Work Orientations* (Washington, D.C.: The Brookings Institution, 1972).

firms, offer almost no career opportunities, and suffer dispropor-
tionally from seasonal unemployment. But theorists bypass the
fact that such jobs in the marginal or "peripheral" sector of the
economy are indispensibly related to the larger economy; larger,
stabler employers in almost all industries depend on the low cost
"secondary sector's" output.

These jobs are not likely to disappear, but to increase in their
number as primary sector employers, after the fashion of Japanese employers, evade unions by contracting with vendors to
supply more and more sub-assemblies that can be fitted to their
final products. "Secondary sector" jobs cannot be more attractive,
so to say, than they are—their marginal qualities are, most advan-
tageously, part and parcel of the putative efficiences of the larger
economy. In any event, these jobs require a great deal of "voluntary turnover";[12] it is just a mite disingenuous, under these circumstances, to find much fault with youths "gravitating" toward
these jobs and occupying them "unstably." Ironically, when the
(large) numbers of young Americans accused of rejecting these
jobs lead to shortages in the economy, overall, we blame them for
their lack of patience and their unrealistic expectations—and,
more or less self-righteously turn to "undocumented" workers to
get the job(s) done.

One may, of course, be unsympathetic to Piore's fundamental
point, but it is surprising that bona fide scientists would disregard
what is almost precisely one-half of the evidence about youths in
the labor market, even in the worst of economic circumstances.
Thus, the Bureau of Labor Statistics informed us, during the
earliest days of 1983, that male black teenage unemployment
reached 50 percent in December of 1982; the glass, we may
pessimistically conclude, is half empty. But the labor supply thesis
neglects the fact that 50 percent of all black male labor force
participants age 16–19 are employed; the half empty glass is, by
definition, half full. These two halves are matched on almost all
their human capital traits, a fact that should cause us to disaggre-
gate demand factors rather than to aggregate on the supply side, a
matter to which we will return, momentarily.

---

[12]Michael Piore, "Unemployment and Inflation: An Alternative View," in M. Piore,
Ed. *Unemployment and Inflation: Institutionalist and Structuralist Views* (New York:
M. E. Sharpe, Inc., 1979), pp. 11–12.

It is simply not a creditable scientific position, furthermore, that all, or even most, of the unemployed members of the teenage group, were they hired as a consequence of economic expansion, would be so much less productive than their employed peers that they would force a change in the equilibrium unemployment rate in an inflationary direction. The lower unemployment rates of black male teenagers in Nashville, Tennessee, for example, in accord with the labor supply thesis' central premise, must be taken either as evidence of these workers' productivity or of managerial malfeasance.

Fifth, let us at the very least take note of a conventional alternative to analyses of unemployment and inflation, with their problematical assumptions about the productivity of the unemployed, that wages do not "function" to equate supply and demand. Thus Piore, and John Dunlop before him, have argued that wage rates "define the relationships between labor and management, between one group of workers and another, among various institutional entities [the locals in a national union, the various branch plants of a national company, the major employers in a local labor market, the major international union] ... and last, the place of individuals relative to one another in the work community, in the neighborhood, and in the family."[13] In this view of what is termed their "contours," wages are compared invidiously, one group's with those of one or more other groups. The perceptions stemming from these "coercive comparisons," according to some reputable labor economists, will trigger efforts by the lower-wage workers to catch up with their *socially* defined comparison groups—to restore differences, as Piore puts it— "when shock to the inter-group relationships occur, as when firemen succeed in achieving parity with policemen in our large cities." The marginalist model, relating earnings to productivity, makes little room for institutional realities.

There is considerable support for Piore's position in a study of my own, in the late 1970's, of the work dissatisfactions of a national probability sample of employed Americans. There was, for example, an appreciably more robust association between respondents' overall dissatisfactions with their *jobs* and their

---

[13]Michael Piore, "Unemployment and Inflation: An Alternative View," in Piore, *op. cit.*, p. 6.

envy of the rewards accorded to *others* in *other occupations* than between their overall dissatisfactions with their jobs and their dissatisfactions with what their *own* employers paid them or otherwise did or did not do in the job setting.[14]

My data on this point, incidentally, are apposite because Piore's, and Dunlop's analyses before him, were often based on case studies—interviews and observations—that do not produce data on continuous variables amenable to statistical treatment. As Piore points out (in a plea for patience with studies suggesting that subsets of labor markets are more or less insulated from each other in *dis*continuous fashion), these studies discomfit many of us who cultivate an "aesthetic of continuity"; we harbor deep misgivings about data in which there are discontinuities—as between and among wage contours.[15] Next, when I examined the work dissatisfactions of workers whose educations exceeded the amount "actually" required to perform their jobs, in accord with estimates by Labor Department job analysts, I discovered that the better-paid "underutilized" were considerably more satisfied than the lesser-paid "underutilized workers." Employers, in *addition* to paying for the productivity of workers whose educations I conceive (by reasonable if not totally dispositive criteria) to be underutilized, must thus pay an additional premium to "buy off" dissatisfactions that will occur in the absence of the premium.

In our society, with slow changes in job demands attributable to technological change but with mounting educational achievements, it would be interesting to plot the contribution, in the fashion of the Phillips Curve, of the costs of buying off job dissatisfactions to the annual rate of wage inflation. These costs might also be applied as discounts to the social rate of returns to education since, quite clearly, the premiums are specifically *not* rewards for the productivity putatively produced by education.[16]

Data on the employment experiences of youths are not the

---

[14]See Ivar Berg, *Managers and Work Reform: A Limited Engagement* (New York: Free Press, 1978), Ch. 7.

[15]M. J. Piore, "Labor Market Segmentation Theory: Critics Should Let Paradigm Evolve," *Monthly Labor Review,* Vol. 106, No. 3 (April, 1983), pp. 26–28).

[16]The argument, we should note, that more satisfied workers are necessarily more productive has *not* been proven. For a review, see Ivar Berg, *Managers and Work Reform: A Limited Engagement* (New York: Free Press, 1978), Part I.

only ones that cause one to have some reservations, at least, about conventional treatments of worker productivity. Professors Bibb and Form, for example, have shown that women in blue-collar occupations earn lower wage returns for each year of educational achievement than their peers among blue-collar men, a finding that flies fairly directly in the face of arguments about the critical role of the most basic of the human capital traits contemplated in labor supply theses. What is one to make of a thesis that is based, in one part, on one-half of the teenage labor force participants and, in a second part, on analyses that beg questions about earning differences between the sexes? We should be modest about our claims to be scientists in pursuit of a general theory if we are really considering *only* unemployed teenage labor market participants of given educational achievements and the productivity of the educations, essentially, *only* of males.

We may note, too, in passing, that many labor market supply-human capital theses' advocates are inclined to blame unions for making wage demands in excess of workers' productivity gains. Of particular interest, these days, given our concerns with inflation, are cost-of-living allowances, in "COLA" clauses, in labor-management agreements. These clauses assure that many union members' hourly wages will be pegged, or "indexed," to periodic increases in the rate of inflation as measured by the Bureau of Labor Statistics. COLA agreements, it may surprise younger labor supply theorists to learn, were *not* invented by unionists, however, nor were they indeed initially even much *favored* by unions! As *Business Week* reminded its readers, on December 21, 1982, former General Motors Chairman Charles E. Wilson first proposed "wage escalation," *in 1948,*

> *...as a tradeoff for longer-term contracts and the resulting predictability in labor relations. But inflation was rising at an annual rate of only 1 percent to 2 percent,... the double-digit inflation of recent years has drastically changed the nature of the original bargain. COLAs in the current G.M. and Ford contracts alone will total about $2.55 per hour. (p. 83)*

In *1958,* meanwhile, the United Automobile Workers proposed a profit sharing plan to the automakers, but the plan was rejected by their managers until 1982, as a way, in the much later year, of tying wages to performance and as a way of undoing COLAs. As

Business Week recalls, auto industry leaders, one quarter of a century ago viewed profit sharing "as counter to the U.S. 'capitalist system.'" Manager's behavior is rational in these events; they simply respond realistically to the facts of life in the economy.

When we wish to understand their employees' changing fortunes, however, we must reach out to the field of demography and study the faulty speculations of young workers' parents, the irrational characters of legislators who pass minimum wage laws, and the flawed logics of unionists who don't synchronize their demands with those of the rationalists on the other side of the bargaining tables. If managers do things at "T_1" that appall us at "T_2" as in the case of COLAs, we simply neglect the fact and pronounce retroactive curses on their antagonists.

I may also note in passing, that when the American Association of University Professors publishes its annual study of the economics of the profession, the published results speak always to the matter of the lag of professors' salaries behind inflation. The word productivity is studiously avoided by colleagues in the annual reports. We don't contribute to but suffer from inflation, whatever the declining returns to our former students' educations might suggest about our productivity.[17]

Sixth, consider that most (not all) of the tax incentives and kindred subsidies, including "shadow," or off-budget items, enacted in recent years by Uncle Sam in response to business leaders' urgings, have enjoyed the support of the many among those, especially in Conservative circles, implicitly or explicitly espousing the labor market supply thesis. The evidence, however, does not show that the payoffs on the employment side have been as large as promised over the years. Thus my Vanderbilt collaborators in the aforementioned study-in-progress have examined different industries' capacities to produce employment opportunities, here and abroad, and they have discovered that industries' domestic job production rates were *inversely* related to the amounts of benefices afforded them, directly or indirectly, by a variety of public policies. A few hints about the reasons for these results will be uncovered, we may reasonably suppose, in forth-

---

[17] For a description of higher education's gains from and contributions to inflation, see the author's "The Effects of Inflation on and in Higher Education," *The Annals,* Vol. 456 (July, 1981), pp. 99–110.

coming studies of the contributions of these incentives to mergers and acquisitions.

Seventh, a careful analysis of Phillips Curve calculations can only leave one skeptical about the meanings of the so-called trade-offs they bespeak, trade-offs that are taken to be axiomatic in the loosely formulated proofs tendered in support of the current version of the labor supply thesis. The argument relates, we may recall, to the allegedly low productivity and thus the potentially inflation-producing performance of the largest numbers of the unemployed population were they added to the nation's payrolls as a result of "aggregate demand policies."

David Wheeler, in a neglected paper prepared for the National Committee for Full Employment[18], comments on what appear to be two fatal flaws in the statistical work from which Phillips Curve devotees have regularly reassured themselves about the soundness of their larger model. "The result [of these flaws]," Wheeler writes, "has been the assignment of illusory importance to the unemployment rate as a determinant of wage inflation." He goes on to point out that, while the Phillips Curve postulates a one-way causal relationship from prices to wages, one really must include, in such equations, "as *an inevitable simultaneous counterpart* an equation which identifies wage inflation as *one* cause of price inflation," a problem econometricians refer to as "the simultaneity problem." (Emphasis added.)

The second problem, he urges, is linked to the fact that "the current rate of wage inflation is in part determined by its own past values. ... Past wage inflation generates past price inflation, which in turn contributes to the formation of the present price expectations and the present rate of wage inflation," a dependency problem that is familiarly known to the cognoscenti as lagged endogenity. Simple estimation techniques like those used in the construction of the Phillips Curve "... were never designed to take account of the additional technical problems" created when neither simultaneity nor lagged endogenity are taken into account.[19]

The first of the two issues that Wheeler joins apparently has

---

[18]David Wheeler, "Is There a Phillips Curve?" in M. Piore, Ed., *Unemployment and Inflation: Institutionalist and Structural Views* (White Plains, N.Y.: M. E. Sharpe, Inc., 1979), pp. 46–57.
[19]*Ibid.*, p. 55.

been accorded growing attention, but only a little attention has focused on the problem of lagged endogenity. Compensatory techniques, meantime, have been invented by Professor Ray Fair at Princeton. When Wheeler applied Fair's suggested corrections to Professor Wachter's estimates, he found that:

> ... a 4 percent unemployment rate could be bought for 4.5 percent annual wage inflation. By 1975, things had apparently improved to the point the same [low] unemployment rate could be purchased for an annual rate of 1.6 percent.... Again, the curve itself can only be understood once it is recalled that it represents that part of wage inflation which can be traced to the strength of demand in the labor market. A concurrently high rate of inflation from other sources is perfectly possible, with a resulting sizeable increment to the total observed rate of wage inflation from the impact of inflationary expectations... the important question here is whether the unemployment rate *itself* has had any measurable consequences for inflation in recent years. The answer given by the correctly estimated wage equation is "very little or none."[20]

Dr. Wheeler's critique of the most typical treatments of unemployment and wage inflation "trade-offs" alerts us to an important simplification in the labor supply approach to unemployment.

Finally, eighth, as we already have emphasized, the structural unemployment thesis in its straight human capital cohort crowding, or its earlier technological/structural change phases holds that the high unemployment rates of youths relate not to their youth, per se, but to the modesty of their work experiences and job skills, on the one hand, and their sheer numbers, on the other. Proponents of this view, as we have noted, do not exactly or explicitly blame youthful unemployment victims (or their parents) for their trying circumstances; instead, they simply impute rationality to employers, in the aggregate, who cannot use as many inexperienced workers as are available, because of the baby boom, among labor force participants.

Two of the most lucid presentations of this position, both by Professor Michael Wachter, appeared in Vol. I of the *Brookings Papers on Economic Activity* in 1976, and, in updated fashion, in

---

[20]*Ibid.,* pp. 55–56.

his contribution to these pages. Applying regression techniques to time series data, Professor Wachter showed that teenagers and their slightly older compatriots (through age 24) constituted very large and growing proportions of the population of working-age persons, year by year, over the post World War II era, and that youths' unemployment rates were growing disproportionately higher in each of the years during the same period. Professor Wachter's results were more or less replicated by Joseph Anderson in a widely cited doctoral dissertation at Harvard in 1977.

Louise Russell, a Senior Fellow at Brookings, has urged us to recognize, though, that it is not possible, using Professor Wachter's methods, to truly capture the "baby boom" or the so-called "age structure" effect of which he writes. Dr. Russell proposes that we include the effect of time trends, thereby to force ". . . [Wachter's] age structure measure to prove that it is not standing in for a smooth sequence of changes over time that might have been caused by any number of other factors." A time trend, as she notes, is a standard statistical device for ascertaining whether an alternative factor of interest to an investigator offers a better explanation for patterns observed in a time series than the general flow of events, though she recognizes that if Dr. Wachter's test is insufficiently strict, the time trend test may be a mite too strict. "The basic problem," she writes, "is lack of enough variation in age structure even over a period of 30 years, and it will be solved only when data are available for a much longer period."[21] When such a time trend measure is applied, she reports:

> . . . the coefficient for age structures is no longer positive in any of the equations applied to data on the business cycle and the population share of the young women and men (age 16-17, 18-19 and 20-24) over the period 1947-1980. For men, 18-19 and women 20-24, the coefficient is not only negative but statistically significant, implying that the unemployment rates of these population-subsets are actually lower when young people are a large share of the population.

"Generally speaking," Dr. Russell concludes:

―――――――
[21]Louise B. Russell, *The Baby Boom Generation and the Economy* (Washington, D.C.: The Brookings Institution, 1982), p. 66.

...age structure cannot be distinguished from a smooth trend and thus it is impossible to prove that it is uniquely associated with higher unemployment rates for young workers. ... The fairest conclusion appears to be that, although it is plausible that the unemployment rates of young people are higher when there are more of them, the shortcomings of the time series data make it impossible to derive solid evidence from that source.[22]

Doubts about the interpretations discussed up to this point lead one to look beyond the putative deficiencies of most unemployed Americans and beyond the roles of demographic changes on the distribution of incomes and unemployment in the population. In the next section we move on to consider the possible roles of some economic structures in the generation of unemployment.

Beyond the Human Capital/Structural Unemployment Approach

The first possible adjustments that might be considered, in efforts to get around some of the problems already outlined, have to do with labor markets and other structures affecting employment. The labor supply model, as we have noted, is couched in aggregated demographic terms. In an effort to identify the roles of economic structures, Professors Finegan and Bibb of Vanderbilt University, my collaborators on the investigation I have mentioned earlier, are thus in the closing stages of an analysis in which they have disaggregated unemployment statistics from the 1960 and 1970 dicennial censuses. While they have not yet completed their ecological analysis of the unemployment rates of different population groups in 50 of the nation's Standard Metropolitan Statistical Areas (SMSA's), for example, they report, in working papers, that the changes in the strength of demand for employees overall, in the two time periods, vary such that persons with essentially matched human capital traits face significantly different vulnerabilities in different labor markets. Specifically, some of the differences in the demand for young workers, for example, appear to be explicable by considering

---

[22]*Loc. cit.*

differences in these SMSAs' industry structures and industry mixes.

David Birch, using Dun and Bradstreet data on business *establishments,* reported in 1981, meanwhile, that small (under 100 employees), young (younger than 4 years) establishments with volatile employment records "created" 80 percent of "net new jobs [in his sample]" in 1976. Job losses, without offsetting new jobs, were concentrated in larger establishments.[23] Especially relevant to the present point is the fact that reports based on the Dun and Bradstreet data (on 5.6 million establishments) show remarkable differences in "net job losses" across 10 cities and across four geographical regions—findings that will surprise neither snow belt mayors and governors nor the comparatively more optimistic parents of job-hunting sun belt teenagers.

It should be recognized, though, that Birch's report was based on data for establishments; the conclusions on size must accordingly be treated somewhat gingerly. Thus, while Barry Bluestone and Bennett Harrison, using the same data, recently reported that 88 percent of the 5.6 million establishments in the sample were independently owned, they did not treat these establishments separately from those owned by corporate parents.[24] Following the Bluestone-Harrison report, the Brookings Institution has published additional data, collected by C. Armington and M. Odle, on the relative contributions of small and large business establishments to job creation.

Where Birch's data covered a seven-year period, the Brookings data, separately, cover a two- and a four-year period. Taken together, the Birch and Brookings data suggest: (1) that smaller businesses appear to do better, by way of job creation, over *longer* than over *shorter* periods; (2) that 9 percent of multi-location *firms* (vs. establishments) employ 62 percent of the private sector work force, that many of these are growing, small *establishments* but that, in fact, most of these 9 percent are branches or subsidiaries of large firms; and finally (3) that the contribution to net job growth of "small business" is about proportional to its share of the American labor force. The greater contributions of

[23]David L. Birch, "Who Creates Jobs?" *The Public Interest,* No. 65 (Fall 1981), pp. 3–14.
[24]Barry Bluestone and Bennett Harrison, *Deindustrialization of America: Plant Closings, The Community Abandonment and the Dismantling of Basic Industry* (New York: Basic Books, 1982), p. 27.

small businesses to job creation Birch reports from his data may also stem from the fact that Birch's sample years were relatively more prosperous ones, in cyclical terms, than the two periods studied by Brookings.

These findings are important because they can be juxtaposed with disaggregated data on public policy effects, like those cited earlier from Reich's explorations. My own collaborator, R. Bibb, for example, reports preliminarily that there were *positive* statistical relationships, in his 1960 and 1970 national data, between the tax and other public policy benefits accorded to different industries in these time periods, on one side, and their contributions, so to speak, to the numbers of unemployed of which they were productive, on the other.

Among the most provocative of Bibb's and Finegan's preliminary findings, moreover, was that youth *un*employment rates were *higher* in SMSA's in which retail jobs had *increased*. This finding flies directly in the face of the observation by Professor Wachter and other labor suppliers that youths' jobs grow faster in the retail regions of the service sector wherein neither supervisory nor capital needs are great, wherein part-time jobs proliferate and wherein inexperienced youths' limited skills are less of an occupational hindrance. We cannot yet offer a cogent statistical explanation for what appears to be a contradiction of received wisdom, but my own hunch is that, within SMSA's, retail jobs have expanded only in suburban shopping malls to which part-time and full-time suburban women workers (with cars) have far greater access than do youths from most SMSA's' larger cities.

Mr. Brad Martin, one of Tennessee's prominent real estate developers, reports in a recent conversation that the current "boom" in center cities' commercial redevelopment projects is beginning to offset the suburban mall boom of the past 20 years, in which event youths may regain recently lost claims to a larger share of retail jobs.

A fact not unrelated to those apparently emerging in Finegan's and Bibb's preliminary statistical analyses of inter-sectoral differences in unemployment is that the service sector's productivity rates have gone up.[25] Once again, given the large numbers of

---

[25] See Laura S. Collins, "The Service Economy—What It Means and What It Is" in E. Scheuing, Ed., *The Service Economy* (New York: KCG Productions, 1982).

youths in the service sector, we should stumble over an inconvenient fact—inconvenient because, according to labor supply theorists, we should not expect to find productivity increases where youth work in such significantly large numbers.

Next, we are currently analyzing panel data: (1) from an annual, 11-year-long survey (1968–80) under the direction of James Morgan and his colleagues at Ann Arbor; (2) similar data from 20,000 respondents to a panel survey of seniors in the high school class of 1972 by the National Center for Educational Statistics; and (3) data from 10,000 respondents, over a 10-year period, to a survey, the so-called Parnes data, that has been conducted by labor economists at Ohio State University. Unlike census studies, panel surveys involve repeated interviews with the same respondents over the life of the study.

Our own preliminary results, using only the 1978 data from the Ann Arbor "PSID" files, on respondents' traits, and data on whether they had one or more bouts of unemployment during the period of the panel survey, show that when unemployment is regressed on labor market variables (county, industry, and occupational unemployment rates), they pretty much vitiate the statistical effects of variables descriptive of the individual respondents (family background, ability, years of schooling). The availability of jobs in statistical terms is a significant factor net of job holders' and job seekers' attributes.

While we are not yet ready to report on our analyses of the two other panels, Parnes has conducted a similar analysis of the incidence and duration of unemployment experiences during the period 1966–76 of young male respondents to the Ohio State survey. His results indicate that, while educational differences among these youths are significant in the direction predicted in labor supply studies, these respondents' employment experiences are as much or more influenced by changes in their occupations (within either blue- or white-collar sectors); by their industry's vulnerabilities, statistically speaking, to unemployment; by respondents' changes of employers; and by the number of continuous years they participated in the labor force.[26]

---

[26]Herbert S. Parnes, *Unemployment Experience of Individuals Over a Decade: Variations by Sex, Race and Age,* (Kalamazoo, Mich.: Upjohn Institute for Employment Research, 1982), pp. 5–35 and Table A-3, pp. 69–73.

The panel data we and others are analyzing are of particular interest because they permit the analyst to compare the effects of respondents' *own* individual traits with those of respondents' *own* economic environments, and to do so year by year. Such comparisons, though based on smaller samples than those found in the census files or current population surveys, favored by labor supply theorists, can, of course, be compared and contrasted with the results of these theorists' ecological analyses of data based on larger samples. In their analyses they juxtapose rates descriptive of a particular research population—youths and older workers, for example—with rates descriptive of another variable for the same populations.

But it is clearly an advantage, in the panel data, that one minimizes the risks of committing ecological fallacies. Such panel analyses contrast with an examination of data on the rates of one or another type of experience pertaining to *groups* of teenagers to which one has assigned averages or scores descriptive of their experiences, their personal traits, and their economic-environmental exposures.

In a third effort to elaborate on the more parsimonious but problematic structural unemployment thesis, we used the panel data from Ann Arbor to follow up on a suggestive analyses, by Professor Morgan's Michigan colleagues, of the means by which their respondents had obtained the jobs they held at the time of the 1978 "wave" of the PSID survey. In our version of the job-seeking/job-finding process, we regressed the stability of respondents' employment (the number of years in which they had at least one bout of unemployment, whatever the reason) on measures of the same respondents' personal traits and the economic-environmental exposures that we utilized in the research prongs mentioned in this section. It turns out that third-party intermediaries—i.e., friends and acquaintances familiar with both the persons they sponsor and the employers to whom workers are referred—can help "bond" a job seeker and, through their knowledge of job seekers' qualifications and employers' needs, can more or less match the two. Accordingly, these third-party intermediaries play very significant (which is to say, favorable) roles in determining the employment experiences of 54 percent of white and 58 percent of black respondents in the sample. Those accorded help by third parties enjoy substantially stabler employment records.[27]

While most analysts are aware that personal contacts can provide valuable information to job seekers, we tend to assume, in the labor supply approach, for argument's sake, that youths like other job seekers have essentially equal and fairly extensive labor market information. Our analysis strongly suggests, however, that major differences between youths with many and youths with few bouts of unemployment are related not only to differences in their accesses to what we may think of as "matchmakers" but to differences in the conditions of demand they face in their particular markets and in their industries. Together, these two sets of variables, demands for labor and the availability of third party help, significantly dampen the effects of their personal attributes on their employment experiences. The popular adage holding that, "It's not what you know but who you know," finds considerable support in our data, as does the proposition that, if one doesn't know much about labor markets, in the disaggregated sense, one may read aggregated data on unemployment rather too uncritically.

Persons who have attended high school and who have helpful job contacts will fare better than "drop outs" with such contacts, to be sure. But *within* each of these groups, those with helpers fare far, far better than those without them, a proposition that holds for both blacks and whites. It is possible that many employers are rational, as we commonly suppose in our models, but that their particular brand of rationality does not lead them to discriminate against youths because of this group's *inexperience*. Rather they discriminate *among* youths on the basis of information from bonding agents. Their choices suggest different strategies and tactics than those imputed to them by labor supply theorists, whose models are constructed around differences between youths' and non-youths' labor markets fates, differences that lead the theorists to focus on the different experience levels of the two groups. It is not at all obvious that the differences in the fates of "sponsored workers," compared to those without third-party

---

[27]Janice Shack-Marquez, "Inside Information and the Employer-Employee Matching Process," doctoral dissertation (Philadelphia: School of Public and Urban Policy, University of Pennsylvania, May 1983), p. 18.

bonding agents, bespeak the higher productivity of the former group compared with the productivity of unsponsored workers, especially among younger workers.

Because a good deal has been made of the possibility, despite Goodwin's findings, noted earlier, that unemployed workers suffer their circumstances because their work-related attitudes are flawed, we are analyzing data, on an annual basis, of the work attitudes of the Ann Arbor and Ohio State panels, and it is my expectation that our results will match Goodwin's. Our suspicions that their work attitudes do not contribute much, one way or the other, to the fates of those who suffer "some unemployment" are heightened by the Parnes group's own findings that there were no differences (in 1969) between the cumulative numbers of weeks of unemployment of those young males overall, with "high" and those with "low commitments to work."[28] It may well be that there are differences in our data between the commitments to work of the stably employed and the relatively few who suffer the most incidences and longest spells of unemployment, but we are wagering that these commitments decline in consequence of their labor market experiences, statistically speaking, as labor markets variables have increasing weight; we do not expect to observe, in annual panel data, that problematic attitudes precede problematic experiences, though at some point there may well be cross-over points such that a string of sad experiences provoke reactions which contribute, in a subsequent period, to further sad experiences. Fortunately, there are biometric techniques for examining discrete events over time.

Conclusion

The net values of the research tactics we are pursuing, above and beyond those employed by the labor supply/human capital/structural unemployment theory's protagonists, should be viewed as augmentations of our colleagues' efforts. But even when we synthesize all these data, we are not likely to be able to go very far down better public policy paths. The simple fact is that, while our added terms, pertaining to labor markets, have

---

[28]H. Parnes, *op. cit.*, p. 72.

added very significantly to the predictive powers of equations containing both "our" and "their" favored terms, the *total* variance in the phenomenon to be "explained" tends to be very small in our studies, if a mite larger than in those conducted by proponents of the labor supply approach. Other investigators' works, in which labor market data and related data on economic structures are considered together with data on workers' personal traits, have not had much better fortunes than we have experienced.[29]

The large unexplained residuals, reported in a host of studies, suggest that social scientists in this area, not less than such other substantive fields of study as crime or mental illness, work some distance away from the kinds of lean models available in physics and chemistry; workers' experiences are quite obviously influenced by factors and forces that are simply not captured even in the more complicated multivariate models of employment and unemployment. Much more, however, may well be learned about the potent roles *vis a vis* unemployment of factors identified in other areas of sociological investigations, especially studies of intra-organizational phenomena and, related to the human capital model, a cluster of studies, like those by the Dreebens, at Chicago, of what, indeed, goes on in the governance and operations of the nation's schools; "years of schooling," after all, is a fairly poor surrogate measure of what schools impart to youths.

Consider, as one example, that we have literally thousands of studies of the effects on worker productivity of different organizational structures and of the effects on workers or the work norms, for example, of the groups to which workers belong in their work places. Similarly, economists and sociologists have published many studies of the consequences for work performance of race and sex discrimination, containing results to which, for reasons of space limitations, no attention has been paid in this paper.

It is customary to end papers like this one with a section suggesting what the author would commend by way of public policymaking, a custom I will honor only briefly.

My disposition is to say that we should call moratoria: (1) on claims that there is, at any given moment, *an* "equilibrium unemployment rate"—i.e., an unemployment rate compatible with

---

[29]For a fair sampling, see the articles by contributors to Ivar Berg, *Sociological Perspectives on Labor Markets* (New York: Academic Press, 1981).

stable inflation and below which increased inflation will occur; and (2) on the related claims that, therefore, we must eschew "aggregate demand policies" targeted on the production of additional job opportunities in the so-called private sector.

These pages, I finally hope, will inspire a few labor supply enthusiasts among my colleagues to consider, at least, that shifts in observed equilibrium unemployment rates are longitudinal *measures* of the statistical relationships between a pair of important variables. Accordingly, they should not be treated as reciprocal *causes* of each other's movements and, thereafter, as definitive guides to policy.

We may not know anywhere near as much as we would like to know about the vexed productivity-inflation nexus. Nonetheless, it can only be damaging to our social fabric to consign whole demographic groups to subsets of persons simply labelled as productive or unproductive on the basis of the means, modes, and medians descriptive of a population's personal traits that are then juxtaposed with their earnings and employment records. Available data simply do not confirm the legitimacy of such labelling exercises because the label too often derives from analyses that appear to involve the fallacy of insufficient statistics and the causal fallacy long known as *post hoc ergo propter hoc.*